SHARON AND HERB GLASER

GOD AND FREUD

by Leonard Gross

DAVID McKAY COMPANY, INC.   New York

Gross, Leonard. God and Freud. New York, D. McKay Co. [1959]
    215 p.   21 cm.   1. Psychology, Religious.   2. Pastoral psychology.
    3. Freud, Sigmund, 1856–1939. I. Title. BL53.G78   201
    59–6696 ‡   Library of Congress

MANUFACTURED IN THE UNITED STATES OF AMERICA

VAN REES PRESS • NEW YORK

For Jackie

CONTENTS

vii

GOD AND FREUD

1.

THE CHANGING BELIEF

O N A steaming day in Chicago one recent summer a student at the Illinois Institute for Juvenile Research was drawn from his work by a fascinating scene below. Emerging at a run from the building, a psychiatrist named William J. Devlin was tucking a brilliantly flowered sports shirt into a pair of black pants. That done, Devlin, a husky, bursting man of fifty, then tied the white collar and black rabat of a Roman Catholic priest to his person, slipped into a priest's single-breasted black coat, and ran off to a nearby church to say a mass.

Caught in flight, Father and Doctor Devlin, S.J. and M.D., symbolizes a fascinating movement developing today within most of the important religious institutions in the United States. The movement is an outgrowth of a volatile courtship between two once-hostile disciplines concerned with the acts and moods of men—religion and psychiatry.

Fifty, forty, thirty, and even twenty years ago anyone who suggested that religion and psychiatry would ever "get together" would have been considered mad by both. To the great body of clergy in the United States, psychiatry was an insidious foreign plot to wreck the Church. Sigmund Freud, a Jew from Vienna, received all the abuse of a man trying to make off with the collection plate. To many psychiatrists, on

the other hand, religion was an antiquated illness that had
fettered man for centuries and, in the light of modern needs
and knowledge, could no longer be tolerated.

These views remain, but they are dying just as surely as
their progenitors. In less than a lifetime, the coming together
of new science and old faith has become one of religion's most
significant modern trends. Like Father Devlin in that swift
summer moment, the activity engendered by this encounter is
headlong, intriguing, dynamic, potent, and one of the greatest
seeming contradictions of our time.

This is a movement in which a Protestant minister has listened without protest as a woman called God a son of a bitch,
then worked unceasingly with the blasphemer until her faith
was restored.

This is a movement in which another Protestant minister
has baptized the infant of a woman who had been living with
a married man, on the grounds that baptism could mean
psychological and religious salvation for mother and bastard
child.

This is a movement in which a rabbi-turned-psychiatrist
has taught a Christian to love God; in which a group of chaplains has accepted a psychiatrist's advice not to discuss salvation with a sick man; in which a priest has declared that
Catholic girls who cannot give themselves to men as brides
are too sick to give themselves to Christ as nuns.

It is a movement that extols psychiatry, the recent villain,
as the hero of a great new chapter in religious life. More and
more clergymen, particularly those ordained in recent years,
now credit psychiatry as having awakened them to the dynamic resources of their own faith; as having turned abstract
idealism into practical reality; as having given useful meaning
to the divine concepts of love, forgiveness, acceptance, and
understanding.

It is, conversely, a movement that is damned and vilified not only by some psychiatrists, who accuse clergymen of attempting to practice medicine without license, but by some clergymen, who accuse their impassioned brethren of forsaking theology for science.

For all its controversy, the movement to incorporate the new science with ancient theology has been inextricably blended into the much-advertised religious revival in the United States, and in the opinion of some authorities accounts for a good part of the enthusiasm with which many Americans, emerging from a period of religious skepticism, are embracing their faiths today.

When two once adamantly antagonistic bodies get together, it is fair to ask whether one has changed the other in any basic way. With all the activity, study, and discussion under way about the emerging dimension of man, what has happened to the religious organizations to which more than one hundred million Americans profess belief? Have they a new look? A new tone? A new manner of interpreting old truths? While it is nice enough to contend, as clergymen do, that religion and psychiatry are in "the same business," it is one thing to say, as some religions do, that God is the heaven and the earth, and another to say, as some psychiatrists do, that God is a creation of the mind—a "father figure" who looks or acts like one or the other parent, or both.

The truth is that whereas religion and psychiatry have been exchanging uneasy platitudes about how they can "get along," "live in harmony," and "enrich one another" while staying out of each other's way, psychiatry has actually made such a deep impression on some religious groups that a sheep returning to the fold after some years of separate grazing might have trouble recognizing the flock.

If he is returning to such an affected church out of a specific need, a parishioner will find resources to help him that were simply unavailable years before. If his particular church is one that has been severely bitten by the urge to ally with the new science of man, he might at first wonder whether he hasn't walked into a family guidance center, or, in extreme cases, a psychiatric clinic itself. In most "modern" or "progressive" churches he will surely find a minister ready to give him counsel who has been trained in the insights of depth psychology and, in a small but expanding number of cases, has himself been analyzed. Under ideal conditions this minister is prepared to deal with his parishioners' problems until he has helped them or until he sees that his own resources are inadequate to the need and refers the parishioner to competent psychiatric help.

The returning member might find himself drawn to a session in "group dynamics" with other members. If an Episcopalian, he might find himself at an emotionally charged "parish-life conference" where he would watch lifelong churchgoers stunned by realizing that their failure to accept "unacceptables" in the way that a psychiatrist accepts a sick patient is really pious hypocrisy.

But beyond giving the faithful new insights into the dynamics of their own faith, beyond giving pastors the tools with which to involve themselves as never before with the needs of their flocks, psychiatry, the evidence indicates, has inadvertently transformed certain religious institutions and attitudes in a number of significant ways.

There has been a rejuvenation of the hospital chaplaincy, so that today a chaplain is a respected man in the church hierarchy and not—as he so often was thirty years ago—a chap who would "get a parish" once his luck had turned.

There has been a major overhaul of Sunday-school curriculums and teaching methods in many churches, sometimes with the direct assistance of psychiatrists and psychologists, but invariably with the aim of incorporating psychiatric insights.

There has been an increasing reliance on psychiatrists and psychological testing devices to screen out of divinity schools candidates for the priesthood, ministry, or rabbinate whose inspirations are neurotic rather than spiritual.

Then, granting that there has been a considerable amount of poor theology in this country in which, to the despair of enlightened theologians, religion has been twisted out of all resemblance to definitive church doctrine, there is evidence that where there have been distortions and where psychiatric insights have been brought to bear, many distortions have been put to rout.

Some clergymen have come to believe that they have been so concerned with enforcing morality that they have used God as an instrument of discipline and have thus obscured the message of God's love—a message basic to Christianity and Judaism and evident always in many churches and synagogues without any hand from psychiatry.

Certain clergymen influenced by psychiatry and having an authoritarian past now admit that in acting as moral policemen they have created anxiety and insecurity among some of their congregants. They go even further. They blame this misplaced emphasis on a religion of legalism as one source of intolerance and interchurch squabbling, feeling that such bigotry often serves as an emotional outlet for insecure people.

In churches where these admissions are being made the antiquated image of God as a towering, vengeance-wreaking old man, discarded by many theologians as a distortion over the past fifty years, is at last being effectively cast aside by grass-roots congregations, to be replaced by the historically elusive image of the deity as a God of love—an image with equal or even greater theological validity. Says the Reverend A. T. Mollegin, a highly respected teacher and biblical scholar of the Protestant Episcopal Theological Seminary in Alexandria, Virginia:

"For many people in many traditions there has been—as a consequence of the influence of depth psychology—a recovery of understanding that love and forgiveness are more fundamental and basic than condemnation. The whole psychologic category of acceptance has illumined and emphasized the idea of divine forgiveness. Witness the acceptance by Christians and Jews of the sinners in their midst. They know now that they must accept a sinner as a real person, no matter what he's done. This is the beginning of redemption. People learn that this was in their basic theology all the time. Depth psychology—call it what you will, call it psychiatry— has helped us overcome moralistic condemnation so rampant in fundamentalist groups."

The acceptance of these ideas by clergymen who have not previously held them has caused them to undergo what one of their number described as "an agony of re-evaluation," not only of their own beliefs, but of their roles as well. Clergymen who once fancied themselves sole custodians of God's word and who judged and condemned on this assumption have come to believe that the most important thing they can do for their congregants is that which numbers of their own enlightened colleagues have been doing all the time—to listen, understand, and forgive.

In hand with reawakened concern for individual problems has come another development whose significance will be measurable perhaps only years from now. There has been a re-examination by some clergymen of the manner in which they have been interpreting moral codes, and an admission that in some instances they have been secularizing standards of conduct out of all relation to pure church doctrine. "It was a new idea to me when I came to this country that drinking, smoking, and dancing were religious issues," says English-born George T. Hedley, a Methodist minister and member of the Mills College faculty in Oakland, California. "Religion in America is really much more strict—more puritanical—than elsewhere."

Behavior that some clergymen have historically dealt with as "sin" they now treat as "symptom." Says a Southern California clergyman, W. R. Hall, "What may have been sin when I was a boy we would now consider an illness for which the man has no responsibility." A man who drinks too much, in other words, may not necessarily be wicked. He may be sick.

Most striking in this area, perhaps, is the re-examination of ethics being undertaken by a progressive element in United States Protestantism, the group most deeply affected by the age of psychology. Where other educated religious groups contend that standards of sin are unchanged, this small but intellectually potent Protestant element, whose most luminous figure is the renowned theologian, Paul Tillich, wonders whether sin can ever be anything other than "estrangement from God." Members of this group are seeking approaches to such aspects of sexual activity as masturbation, premarital intercourse, marriage, adultery, and divorce that they consider true both to modern scientific understanding and to the most authentic spirit of Christianity. It is their contention that this ethic may turn out to be vastly different from what is considered "Christian" today. On the basis of a thorough restudy of the theology of sex in the light of contemporary understanding, this group contends that today's prevalent religious morality is both "unbiblical and antibiblical."

The final concomitant of the religion and psychiatry adventure is a deeply philosophical one, involving a search for new definitions of original sin, the hereafter, and God that, instead of sometimes confounding man, bear more directly on his life.

To suggest that belief is changing is to invite attack, especially if the contention is that the change is in response to a force that is itself a target of attack. Yet religion has always been affected by the eddies and currents of contemporary tides. As sociologist Samuel Blizzard, perhaps the foremost student of clerical life in the United States, suggests, clergymen have always responded to secular forces. "They are famous for their ability to attach themselves to another profession," he notes. "Since the turn of the century they have successively looked to social workers, educators, and now clinical psychologists and psychiatrists to help them out." While little popular attention has been given to the possibility that religion has been undergoing a significant change in the last fifty years as a result of psychiatry's challenge, is it not possible that psychiatry has made as deep a mark on theology as it has on society in general? It seems incredible that religion could have remained an impregnable bulkhead to these dynamic tides, that its shores would have remained unwashed and unchanged. In the light of the facts it is insupportable.

While psychiatry has not invented any ideas about love and forgiveness that had not been expressed by religionists centuries before, there can be no denying the feelings of countless clergymen that psychiatry has made their faiths more alive and authentic than ever before. Indeed, while this foment has largely escaped public attention, it is viewed by Theologian Tillich as a development that, historically, will ultimately match in significance the period of St. Augustine.

Which is to estimate, as does Psychiatrist Earl Loomis, that "religion may never be the same again."

2.

"GOOD RELIGION AND GOOD PSYCHIATRY ARE IDENTICAL"

IN MANY religion-and-psychiatry circles today it is smart to say that Sigmund Freud was a religious man.

To anyone with even a casual interest in the doctrines that made Freud one of the most significant men in history, the thought of a religious Freud comes as quite a surprise. In both conversations and writing Freud left an ample record of his conviction that organized religion was a "neurosis" that cost man dearly.

From what he had learned of his patients, Freud decided that man seeks in God the security he knew as a child. In his earliest years man had a father who protected him, provided for his needs, and solved his problems. Older and alone, his father gone, man yearns for the security of his childhood. Lacking a God, he would create one in the image of his own father. Having one, he is once again comfortable, knowing he will be cared for. But he has paid a fearful price. Though he might sustain himself in the face of the frightening demands of living, he has regressed to the level of a child. He has abdicated his desire for greatness. Furthermore, he has surrendered to a paralyzing belief. Rather than relying on his reasoning powers, he now accepts ideas on faith. By stifling his critical faculties, he aborts his intellectual growth.

One other characteristic of religion irked Freud, and that was its implication that goodness was the exclusive property of the devout. If this is true, a Freud interpreter, Erich Fromm, notes, then what of the people who don't believe in God? They would run wild. "If the validity of ethical norms rests upon their being God's command, the future of ethics stands or falls with the belief in God. Since Freud assumes that religious belief is on the wane he is forced to assume that the continued connection of religion and ethics will lead to the destruction of our moral values." [1]

As if these criticisms of religion were not enough to send religious professionals to the guns, there were two rudiments of Freudian psychoanalysis that most religionists, at the time, considered blasphemous.

In developing an explanation to cover all human behavior, Freud decided that all of us don't always act as we think we will, or even think we should. This hidden force he called the "unconscious." It is a sort of depository for significant memories dating from very early life, memories that we can't consciously recall but that remain with us nonetheless because they were and are significant in determining our personality.

The concept of an unconscious raised a basic and vital conflict between religious and psychiatric notions about people that in some cases may never be resolved. When a man commits adultery, or beats his children, is he wicked, or is he acting for reasons he doesn't understand? Religion in the main holds that man has the free will and moral responsibility not only to choose a righteous course of

[1] *Psychoanalysis and Religion* (New Haven: Yale University Press, 1950), p. 13.

conduct, but to pursue this ideal consistently. Freud said that man is much too complicated to account consciously for everything he does.

The second Freudian rudiment that enraged religion was the now historic libido theory. All human conduct, the psychiatrist said, can be explained in terms of the sexual drive. And by "all" he meant exactly that. Not only adults were susceptible to devious, frequently hidden drives for sexual release, but infants as well. To take just one example, the child nursing at his mother's breast is engaged, according to Freud, in a sexual act, and the process of weaning is no less violent an experience for him than the frustration of a passionate love for an adult.

Quite naturally, Freud's theories of sex were an affront to religious groups. If he was right, then the religious theories about what constituted a "decent" man seemed suddenly to be wrong. Even more to the point, if one accepted Freud, religious conceptions of sexual morality appeared to be completely unrealistic. And if religion could sucessfully be charged with the possession of an impossible set of standards of conduct, the next step, inevitably, was its dethronement. Obviously, Freud was the devil's disciple.

But if you look hard enough in the worst imaginable clutter, you are bound to find something good. And in psychiatry, religion found something very good indeed.

The uniting discovery was the power of a single word: love. Love is not just pretty, or nice, or holy, or good, as religion seemed to be saying. Love, psychiatry proved with overpowering drama, is as essential to sane existence as food. Its absence creates a void into which rush fear, then hate.

Without love a man can become awesomely, terribly violent, and for proof, religion needed only to witness these cases taken from its own ranks:

A fourteen-year-old boy batters a sixty-five-year-old woman

he has never seen before because she unconsciously reminded him of the grandmother who had reared him but never loved him.

A man attacks his wife with a hatchet because her aggressiveness invokes the memory of his aggressive father, who never loved him. Said a case study: "He was really taking a hatchet to his father."

A mother, informed that her severity is making her daughter uncertain of her love, runs home and beats the child until the child cries, "Yes, Mommy, I know you love me."

In dramatic and convincing terms psychiatry was talking religion's language. "God is love ... God loves ... God will love, if ..." is, however much it may be neglected or forgotten from time to time, the great attraction of all successful, significant Western religion. "Love" was the idea you supposedly heard every time you went to church. Love was your reward for being good. Even if you had been bad, love could be yours if you confessed your sins and vowed to be better. The sin is wicked, never the sinner. God *accepts you* for what you are.

More convincingly than anything else ever had, *the psychiatric method dramatized the religious idea of acceptance.* The primary step in helping an emotionally ill person is to make him believe that he is a person who counts, a person about whom someone cares. No matter what he has done, the psychiatrist wants to help him get well. The psychiatrist does not condemn him, and is not disgusted with him.

This absolutely basic tenet of psychiatric treatment does not mean that every psychiatrist is automatically a saint the day he begins to practice. It does mean that if he wants to be a successful psychiatrist he has got to accept people who are living life wrong and who, in many ways, are undesirable—that is, unlovable. In effect, he has got to *love the unlovables.*

Loving the unlovables is perfect religion, and that is why one of the most frequently heard expressions among psychiatrically oriented clergymen around the country is that, in this one significant respect, "good religion and good psychiatry are identical."

Wherever "good religion" was not being exercised, and wherever the religionists involved took a look at psychiatry, this is the precise point at which they caught their breath.

How many times in their sermons had these clergymen talked about the wrath of God without mentioning God's love? How often had they preached the Word, without bothering to listen to the worries of parishioners? Did they have any idea that while they would cry "Love thy neighbor!" a parishioner might be wondering, as one mental hospital chaplain puts it, "Why the hell can't I?"

"Traditional Christianity," comments Author-theologian Reuel L. Howe, "has talked about the love of God endlessly while its parishioners were dying from problems in their love life."

Even more significant than the lack of consideration for the individual, perhaps, was the emphasis upon creed. Religionists themselves can be most acid on this score, and the late David E. Roberts noted frankly a few years ago that "Protestantism, while generally stressing salvation through trust, forgiveness, and grace, as a matter of doctrine, has all too often tended to turn the Christian life into a moralistic struggle toward an abstract, perfectionist goal as a matter of practice. Some of its teachings even sound as though the only way to be driven into an acceptance of the love of God involves first being paralyzed by dread of his wrath." [2]

One other factor was instrumental in bringing religionists

[2] *The Church and Mental Health,* edited by Paul B. Maves (New York: Charles Scribner's Sons, 1953), p. 28.

closer to psychiatry. Many clergymen acknowledge freely today that they had somehow become office managers during the week and orators on the weekend. Religion, for ministers especially, had lost its holiness, and had lost sight of people. Clergymen had become anxious to restore a sense of usefulness to themselves. They wanted pre-eminently to be "pastors" once again to their flocks. In the new science they saw their agent. "Psychiatry, properly used in the training of a minister, can recapture the ministry from the tea-drinking phase to something useful," one veteran observed.

On several levels, therefore, conditions were ripe for some form of union. Dr. Carroll A. Wise, a Methodist minister and a pioneer in the field, describes the situation simply: "It began to look as if psychiatry had something we could use. So we took a look at it."

The first memorable point of contact occurred in 1925 at the State Hospital in Worcester, Massachusetts, in the form of a program of "clinical training" leading to proficiency in "pastoral counseling." The program was begun by the Reverend Anton T. Boisen, a dedicated minister who had himself recovered from an emotional illness. Pastoral counseling, of course, is as old as the church itself, but this was the first time clergymen had an opportunity to prepare for it scientifically. Young ministers in increasing numbers volunteered to act as orderlies, making beds and emptying bed pans, for the privilege of listening to patients in a psychiatric setting. They wanted to learn what had made these people sick, and the occasion is notable because it involved a use of "listening" rather than "preaching." It didn't matter what they, the young ministers, thought; what mattered was that the sick people told *them*.

Dr. Wise became active eventually in the training phase of pastoral care, but he recalls with some relish his experience when he instituted a pastoral counseling program at a church in Minneapolis. The response was tremendous, despite the fact that most of official churchdom was denouncing psychiatry as "atheistic." When Dr. Wise left Minneapolis there were fifty people waiting to see him whom he had simply not had time for. "Very few people in the church were aware that what I was doing had any connection with psychiatry," he recalls.

The movement of religion toward psychiatry became a classic case of a snowball rolling downhill. Tree stumps were encountered along the way, to be sure, but the velocity was nonetheless terrific. Five years after Dr. Boisen opened his program, the Council for Clinical Training was incorporated in New York City, to become the largest sponsor for ministers' training programs in hospitals and correctional institutions. Seminaries began to send students as part of their training to hospitals and mental institutions for courses in what makes people emotionally sick and gets them well. By 1938 the interest in coexistence was such that when the American Psychiatric Association scheduled a seminar on religion and psychiatry at its annual convention, more than eleven hundred persons besieged a room set up to accommodate fifty.

In the United States today certain popular religionists still make a career out of denouncing psychiatry as the atheistic offspring of the irreverent, iconoclastic Viennese, Freud. Since Freud's pronouncements on religion are less than fifty years old and since the counterattack mounted by clergymen who saw in Freud's criticisms a threat to their existence is even fresher, it is no wonder that lay people generally suppose that undying antagonism still exists between the two groups.

There *is* antagonism, but it becomes less and less fashionable each year. More typical is a statement such as this one made by a Protestant clergyman:

"What we're learning now is really as old as Christ. It took psychiatry to reveal our own religion to us."

More and more commentators within the newly hyphenated area of religion-and-psychiatry are remarking on the "similarities" between the two disciplines. In a sampling of their remarks can be found a sense of the irresistibility of the attraction between them, and the inevitability of their intermingling.

"We're really in the same business, you know," one minister confesses "—helping people." A priest, the Reverend Alexius Portz of St. John's University in Minnesota, acknowledging that there is "a change of mentality on both sides," comments: "In principle science and religion are compatible. Somebody just goofed on the reasoning."

The Reverend Wayne Oates, a leading Baptist advocate of adapting psychiatric insights to religious uses, comments: "I used to feel defensive about some of the psychological criticisms of religion. The more I studied eighth-century prophets and Jesus, the more I realized these guys were saying the same thing."

Some idea of the extent to which psychiatrists and religionists of today are shopping in each other's stores can be seen when we group together just a few of their current attitudes. The outgoing president of the American Psychiatric Association in 1956, R. Finley Gayle, Jr., gave his convention address on the subject, "Conflict and Cooperation Between Psychiatry and Religion." The incoming president, Francis J. Braceland, was the editor of a book of Catholic commentary titled *Faith, Reason, and Modern Psychiatry*. At a convention forum on "Religion, Ethics, and Psychiatry" speakers were declaiming against ministers who try to be psychiatrists and psychiatrists who try to substitute for God. Around the corner in Chicago's Loop the Medical Hospital Chaplains' Association was holding its annual meeting at another hotel. It was no accident that the chaplains had scheduled their convention for the same week as had the psychiatrists.

Seminars bringing together psychiatrists and clergymen are as accepted as political conventions. In the last year alone some fifty were held in cities throughout the United States. Virtually every United States seminary of the first rank now offers a course in "pastoral psychology." In the fall of 1956, for the first time in history, a full-time faculty chair in psychiatry was established at a school of divinity, the influential Union Theological Seminary in New York.

Special departments to supervise clinical training have been established by several leading denominations. An "Academy of Religion and Mental Health" was established in 1954, its purpose to stimulate the amount and quality of clinical training received by clergymen of all denominations; its growth has been phenomenal.

Even the United States Government has entered the field. The Institute for Mental Health, a department of the United States Public Health Service, has granted $426,000 to be shared by Harvard Divinity School, Yeshiva University of New York, and Loyola University of Chicago in establishing courses in mental health.

Today many observers of the religious scene contend that the most enlightened ministers hold the "new view" and are certainly most in demand by congregations looking for a new clergyman. "The old-time theologians have a hard time finding work these days," one rabbi remarks ruefully.

Among ministers it has already become a cliché to say that "Jesus was the first psychiatrist." Another frequently heard remark is that "the churches and the psychiatrists represent the only people who aren't ashamed to use the word 'love.' "

It is impossible to determine exactly how many religionists are using psychiatric insights in their ministry. Samuel Blizzard, the sociologist, who is professor of Christianity and Society at Princeton Theological Seminary, can only "guess" that between 20 and 25 per cent of the Protestant clergy have been affected. Certainly in the Bible Belt of the Deep South the movement has had very little effect, perhaps none at all. Orthodoxy is—and, paradoxically, just as often is not —another limiting factor, and thus within a specific discipline will be found people admitting to the profound effects of psychiatric insights on their religious beliefs, while others of the same denomination whose church might well be in the next neighborhood will damn the trend, instead.

But as Sigmund Freud was followed by significant psychiatrists who described new theories of motivation and did not attempt to tweak the nose of religion, so religion has found itself increasingly more comfortable with psychiatry. Just as psychiatry was an offshoot of psychology, so was psychoanalysis a derivative of psychiatry. Methods of applying the new knowledge that did not rely exclusively on a patient's sexual history or on the dredging up of past problems through extensive analysis came into being. Carl Gustav Jung, the first to break with Freud, stressed the need for emphasis on present difficulties. Then, where Freud's therapy seemed to the religionists to require the liberation of those inhibitions that had been causing guilt, Jung's cure stressed the need for a synthesis by the individual in which he achieved some integration for his life. Alfred Adler emphasized that aims and ideals were a key to the understanding of the individual. Karen Horney, Erich Fromm, and Harry Stack Sullivan all found places for desires other than sex in the composite force that impelled man forward or back. In terms of exploration and subsequent reorientation, religion's role in psychiatric therapy had begun.

With conditions thus improved, the inevitable rapprochement occurred. The ultimate proof of compatibility came from the action of Roman Catholics, the most passionately opposed to psychiatry at the outset and the last to soften their view. While today many Catholics remain adamantly opposed to psychiatry, there is no longer any official support for their attitude. Many are still unaware that in 1953, in a speech to the Fifth International Congress of Psychotherapy and Clinical Psychology, Pope Pius XII declared that while "there are secrets that must on no account be divulged, even to the doctor," the work of the Christian psychologist and psychotherapist was "capable of achieving precious results for medicine, for the knowledge of the soul in general, for the religious dispositions of man and for their development."

Reflecting the initial antagonism, there are far fewer Catholic psychiatrists in the United States today proportionate to church membership than there are Protestants or Jews. But they now number some five hundred and are closing ground rapidly. Even psychoanalysis, once considered anathema because of its intimate concern with an individual's sexual history, is now seen as a useful tool for probing religious beliefs, among other things, to determine what part they play in an individual's illness. Only by discovering neurotic religious attitudes, if they exist, can a psychiatrist assist an individual to a healthy religious approach. Wrote Catholic Psychiatrists James H. Vanderveldt and Robert P. Odenwald:

There need be no opposition between the Catholic religion and analytical psychiatry, so long as the latter avoids smuggling into either its psychological theories or its therapy any philosophical principles that are unacceptable to the former. . . . True, there are psychiatrists who have taken their Catholic patients'

faith away, but there are also others who make better Catholics
out of them by restoring their emotional balance, by making
them more sincere and less egoistic.[3]

The final—and ironic—testimony to the friendship of religion for psychiatry, the fact that closes the circle, is that today
the reputation of Sigmund Freud as a foe of religion is
undergoing considerable softening.

"Freud's belief was really religious," Psychiatrist William
Menninger noted in a conversation a few years ago. "He
believed that love would conquer all hate." Many interpreters now insist that Freud's expressions against religion
were really manifestations of a personal religious problem.
In any case, they say, his "prejudice" should no longer be
considered a part of his psychiatric system, because there is
evidence that he foresaw the day when religion might prof-
itably make use of psychiatric techniques. As proof, these
theorists quote a passage from one of Freud's own books,
The Future of an Illusion, in which he wrote that "the de-
fenders of religion have an equal right to use psychoanalysis
in order to appreciate truly the affective importance of
religious doctrine."

With this interpretation of Freud's attitude toward religion many Freudians would emphatically disagree. It is
quite possible, of course, that religious interpreters may be
picking their evidence because they feel an imperative need
for an alliance. This, after all, is the age of psychology just
as much as it is the age of the automobile, and no contemporary faction attempts to get along without either if it wishes
to remain in the game. Freud is still "the master psychiatrist," Father William C. Bier, S.J., of Fordham University
declares. "His influence in psychiatry is paramount. Indeed,

[3] *Psychiatry and Catholicism* (New York: McGraw-Hill Book Company, Inc.,
1952), pp. 198, 214.

most other psychiatric viewpoints are intelligible largely in terms of their agreement or disagreement with, or divergence from, or modification of, Freud's basic ideas."

Whatever the reason, the results are there. It is no longer unusual to encounter commentary of religionists to the effect that "Freud was really all right; he just went a little too far." Indeed, such is the mood of religion toward its greatest twentieth-century critic that in 1956 at least one prominent church, the Cathedral of St. John the Divine in New York City, found in the centenary of Freud occasion for formal celebration.

And why not? As Psychoanalyst Fromm points out, Freud believed profoundly in the estimable virtues of truth, reason, brotherly love, reduction of suffering, independence, and responsibility.

If that isn't good religion, what is?

3.

THREE MEN

FREUD'S assumption that religion might someday make use of his techniques to explore and enhance its own resources can now be viewed as pure prophecy. In the United States today there are numbers of individuals whose very lives have been given definition by the cross-fertilization of religion and psychiatry occurring for the first time in their age. Perhaps the best way to demonstrate just how far religion has gone to make use of psychiatric insights is to examine three such hybrid individuals. Each of these men is extraordinary and useful because each places a different emphasis on how he wants psychiatry to serve religion. Between the three, therefore, we get a good idea of what is happening, or can happen, to religion as a result of its newest adventure.

WILLIAM J. DEVLIN, S.J., M.D.

He is a richly structured man who gives an immediate impression of immense energy. He smiles at a new acquaintance as though he has known him all his life. His face is striking—he has a grand nose, smallish eyes, and a brow accentuated by baldness—and so, at times, is his dress. A favorite costume is white-on-white shirt, a blue polka-dot bow tie, and a velvet smoking jacket with a bluish cast.

His office is on the eighth floor of Loyola University's downtown campus in Chicago; the door, invariably closed, bears a neat bronze sign on which, no bigger than his signature, is printed his name. Inside there are two deep, deep chairs that leave the ashes of a cigarette a drop of no more than a foot to a big modern ash tray on the floor. The Venetian blinds are drawn against the sunlight, but one weak lamp casts a glow on the ample carpet and the tasteful prints along the walls. Along the far wall is a studio couch with big bolsters at one end and a transparent plastic cover at the other, as though many people are in the habit of placing their feet right there.

They are. William J. Devlin is: (1) a priest; (2) a Jesuit; (3) a doctor of medicine; and (4) a practicing psychiatrist.

His schedule is legendary. He sees between forty and seventy patients a week, some of them two and three times; teaches classes in psychotherapy, psychopathology, and personality development; and from time to time even preaches and conducts retreats. For years he rarely slept, and he once kept himself in shape by running several miles a day with a twenty-five-pound weight on his shoulders.

As one of the first priests ever to become a psychiatrist, his posture seems almost as heroic as his deeds. Actually, he never had any trouble reconciling psychiatry with Catholicism.

"Freud had the right idea operationally—that people act a certain way as a consequence of their experiences and desires," Father Devlin says. "But he used the wrong word. He said sex gave people thrust. That's too simple. It's not true. We say that love or fulfillment—of which sex is only a part—is what gives people thrust."

If this logic is accepted it serves to demolish for Catholics much of the objection they might have to psychiatry and psychoanalysis. Actually, as Father Devlin well knows, the issue is not entirely that simple. The logic does not, after all, do away with sex.

"Look," Father Devlin says emphatically, "when I put on this Roman collar I didn't stop being a man. I have the same drives anyone else has, and nothing anyone vows can ever change that. But if I have drives, I also have ideals— and the ideals can sustain me when I'm tempted by the drives."

This is what Father Devlin means by the "dynamic personality"—the body being the sum of all its parts, with a mind that is influenced by the intestines as well as by religious admonishments. And this is the point at which he is unusually critical of some members of his own church.

"A number of the parish priests don't understand the dynamic personality," he contends. "Some of them are fifty years behind the times. A girl comes to one of them and says, 'Father, I've been sleeping with one of the basketball players and I don't know why.' So he tells her, 'You've sinned, go pray.' Then a man comes to the priest and says, 'Father, I've been drinking too much and beating my wife and I don't understand what I'm doing.' The priest tells him, 'You've sinned, go pray.'

"So you take these guys down to Cook County Psychopathic and you say to them, 'Look, here are three hundred psychotics. A lot of them are Catholics. They've all prayed. Now what?' "

Here, perhaps as pungently as it can be expressed, is the problem of whether an individual has the free will consciously to choose what he wants to do without interference from an unconscious influence of which he is not aware. Catholics believe that although we are sinners by the very fact of our birth, we nonetheless have the free will to select good from bad. Good is divine law, bad is anything else. Thus when one enters a confessional box in a Catholic church he may be very certain that the acts he is admitting to the priest were indeed violations of divine law. But he may be completely oblivious to the real underlying forces that made him do what he did, and he would then be incompetent to answer the priest's question accurately: "Did you know what you were doing when you committed this act?" The sinner might imagine he knew what he was doing, but if his life is being governed by one or more severe emotional injuries he suffered as a child, the acts he committed could be an outgrowth of those forces, and he would not know it unless he had had psychiatric treatment. The young girl, for example, might have been forced into promiscuity to prove to herself that she was worth something, having been cruelly rejected some time before by her parents. The alcoholic may have been overprotected as a child so that in times of crisis as an adult he feels a need for support and turns in desperation to liquor. Neither would *consciously* be aware of why he was doing what he did.

"The moral theologians don't know the dynamic personality," Father Devlin declares. "They've got to understand that people with problems like that girl or that man don't have the free will to make a moral choice, freely based. It's psychiatry's job to help them get rid of their problems so they *can* choose."

And it is the church's job to create a climate in which this process of reconstruction can occur. While sins do not change, there must come "a feeling that you can do something about them," he contends. In this regard, two ideas must be gotten over. Overzealous priests must be taught not to invoke the wrath of God to the extent that they might frighten people into inaction and illness. "I always introduce God as a perfect gentleman," says Father Devlin. Second, he

feels that the Church must show flexibility in administering
its moral codes.

"Look," he explained once, "you know that the Catholic
Church holds marriage to be inviolate, and condemns divorce. But if I can present the picture of a psychopathic personality that was a partner to a so-called marriage but who
didn't have the marrying capacity, didn't have the chassis
or the organization to do what he wanted to do, then I have
proved that this marriage never existed at all. When the
Church can see that the people cannot psychologically accept
the marriage, the marriage is invalid."

To reach that viewpoint Father Devlin has come a long,
long way. The son of a plumber, he was raised in a poor
and tough Chicago neighborhood. At Loyola University,
while earning a straight A average, he won letters in football,
track, and basketball, and served as captain of the basketball
team in his junior year. In that same year, however, he
suddenly quit college cold. In his own words, he was "fed
up with the world" because he saw "no meaning to life." A
few months later, in September 1925, he entered the Society
of Jesus.

For almost twenty years he floundered with magnificence.
He earned six academic degrees, the first four at St. Louis
University. After completing work for his bachelor's, he
took a master's degree in psychology, a subject that bore
directly on his desire to do missionary work in India. When
his appointment to become a missioner came through, he was
sent to Georgetown University to take a special course in
tropical diseases. Returning to Chicago, he found that his
mother, long ill, had just come out of a diabetic coma. His
trip to India was canceled.

While preparing for missionary work, Father Devlin had
also been studying theology. He now returned to St. Louis
University to prepare for his licentiate in philosophy and

in sacred theology. But all the while his thoughts kept
returning to people. Thus when his superiors, determined
that he should go into some sort of special studies, and
having considered psychology, religion, sociology, economics,
and even education, finally left the decision to him, Father
Devlin chose social work.

Transferring to Catholic University in Washington, D.C.,
he obtained a master's degree in psychiatric social work in
1940 and a Ph.D. in clinical psychology in 1942. It was
while earning these degrees that Father Devlin, still dis-
satisfied, found what he wanted at last. With the encourage-
ment of Father Thomas Verner Moore, a psychiatrist who
later became a Carthusian monk, Father Devlin decided
he would become a psychiatrist himself. "I loved people,"
he said, "and I wanted to get on a one-to-one relationship
with my work."

But because he would be the first Jesuit ever to become
a doctor after his ordination, Father Devlin failed to arouse
enthusiasm among his supervisors. They were quite frankly
worried about how the public would react to so unusual a
move.

They sent Father Devlin on a strange mission. For four
years, in between studies, he traveled up and down the
East Coast soliciting opinions from doctors, administrators,
and religious leaders, Catholics and non-Catholics alike.
Recalls Father Devlin: "A few Catholics were for it. Most
of the Protestants were for it. But most Catholics were
against it."

Even so, Father Devlin's pleas finally prevailed. But
when a few individuals who had learned of his intentions
began to criticize him openly to others, Father Devlin's
superior sent to Rome for a dispensation—"just to forestall
any funny business," he recalls. In due course it arrived, a
huge, explicit document, stating that the times demanded

that a priest become a doctor, and that such a priest-doctor
might engage in any sort of medical practice he wished, be
it gynecology, surgery, or psychiatry.

And so, at the age of thirty-eight, the balding father
enrolled in the medical school of the university he had quit
in disillusion twenty years before. His fellow freshman
medical students duly delegated to him the best-looking
cadaver, a young lady known as Suzybelle. In 1947 Father
Devlin obtained his seventh degree, an M.D., *summa cum
laude*. After a year's internship at Cook County Hospital,
a year's residency at the county's Psychopathic Ward and
Neurological Department, and another two years at the Illinois Neuropsychiatric Institute, he was a psychiatrist.

His schedule all this time was nothing less than heroic.
Addicted to wild flowered sports shirts, he frequently wore
them loose over his black priest's pants to facilitate quick
changes when he was to preach or say a mass. He found that
he could stay up for long periods without any sleep at all
easier than getting a few hours' sleep each night. Once,
while on call for surgery duty, he did not go to bed for
three days. He seldom got to bed until 12:30 A.M. and never
rose after four-thirty. Even today, although he has been forbidden to forego sleep because of high blood pressure, he
sleeps little more than half of what a normal man requires.
It is the only way he can see his patients and prepare his
lectures for classes.

The average non-Catholic at some point in his life has
encountered the view that Catholics, because they subscribe
to dogma, are therefore rigid and sententious. The non-
Catholic would never expect to find a Catholic who was
critical of his church, and if this critical Catholic were a
priest, well!

Among sophisticated Catholics, this stereotype has little

relation to reality. Doctrinal argument among some educated Catholics approaches the nature of a pastime; therefore, while Father Devlin is unusual in his criticism, he is by no means unique.

He is, however, refreshingly direct, and this bluntness is a significant part not only of his character but of his relations with others.

He knows he is blunt. Once a priest who had not been doing well in his work was sent to him for treatment. After some period with the man, Father Devlin was convinced that the priest, without realizing it, was manifestly homosexual. It was a ticklish and unpleasant problem, and Father Devlin knew it, for to help the man he had to make him see that he had somehow never resolved the emotional wrench of giving up his mother's breast.

But since the man was a priest, Father Devlin had still another obligation, and that was to enable his superiors to deal properly with the man. After the case was resolved, Father Devlin blurted to a friend:

"I'm the only guy who will go to the Superior and report, 'This person was disturbed in the oral phase, Reverend Holy Father.' "

"This is his appeal," a former student, Dr. Robert Traisman, suggests. "This is what makes him effective. He has a tremendous down-to-earth approach to people and material. You could have someone highly erudite after all those studies and all those degrees. But he remains down to earth. He uses all the words—sex, oral, anal. With people, the gut's the important thing, and he understands the gut."

It is by young people that Father Devlin is most highly regarded. His students worship him, and his young secretary, Barbara Graham, is reluctant to introduce her friends to him because on a few occasions they have ended up as patients. This means overwork, not prosperity for her boss because whatever money he may receive goes to his order.

Among priests themselves, however, there is some question about how Father Devlin is regarded. A psychiatric social worker who was very much *au courant* with developments of this sort told me that Father Devlin had undergone a great deal of persecution by the Jesuits because he had been too forthright in expressing his convictions. When I asked Father Devlin about this, he made an oblique and virtually meaningless reference and positively refused to let me pursue the point.

He does love to shock his colleagues, bursting in upon their meetings with admonishments slightly less than holy, and this habit has not earned him any friends. A close associate suggests that because his training is so extraordinary he feels isolated and a lone wolf, and at times impatient with others who have not had the same educational advantages.

But there is no denying that, on the whole, fellow Catholics are proud of him. In 1955 he was scheduled to speak for an hour to an audience of three hundred in the Red Lacquer Room of the Palmer House. Fifteen hundred priests, nuns, and Catholic psychiatrists turned out for the speech, and after three hours left only because they had to make way for a sports dinner that evening.

On the personal level as well his charm can be devastating. Once in New York we were very late for dinner at the San Marino, a small and extremely popular midtown restaurant. I called, forty-five minutes late, to say that we were on our way, and the furious owner explained that he had held our table almost an hour, and advised us to find another place for dinner. "Don't worry," said Father Devlin, "I'll flash the old collar." So we went, he did, we sat promptly with profuse apologies all around, and several hours later the management bade us good night with a brandy on the house.

There is no denying that Father Devlin is an unusual priest, but it would be a considerable mistake to imagine that he is any less religious or devoted than the most zealous of fathers. He has the same feeling for the Church that a man who is very much in love has for his wife. Annoyed at some imperfection, he will tell her what he thinks, rather than permit the unreleased emotion to eat away at his love.

"Look," Father Devlin explodes, "I've got a woman coming to me who's in her fifties. She's from an absolutely rigid religious background. She thinks God's after her because she's sinned. Her body is rotten—and she's one of the most holy women I've ever met.

"You've got a lot of neurotics that are Catholics. They don't understand that religion is a *service*. You're serving God. But serving means *sharing*—and that's what most people can't do. They never learn that their mothers aren't their exclusive property. They never resolve their Oedipal phase. They never grow up.

"Sixty-five per cent of the people who go to church don't get the true meaning of religion because of afflictions like this. It's my desire to get rid of these afflictions so that these people can get at religion. Only when they grow up can they share, taking less, comfortably, and giving an equal amount back."

Here, he feels, can be psychiatry's contribution to religion —to enable people to worship as he does and feels they can. How can this be brought about? Laments Father Devlin:

"I want my institute."

"The Institute of Child and Adult Living," his greatest dream, would be an outpatient clinic and inpatient residential treatment center set on five hundred acres in the suburbs of Chicago. It would be able to handle the hundreds of emotionally disturbed people he must now turn away.

"I want space," Father Devlin moans. "I can't see kiddies because I don't have space. And I want trainees. I get fourteen, fifteen, sixteen referrals a day. I can't take any more. Where am I going to send these people?"

But in addition to his institute, which could someday rise with the assistance of well-to-do Catholics, Father Devlin is anxious to see the day when parish priests will be well enough trained in depth psychology so that when they take confession they will know when they are listening to a Catholic who is emotionally ill and needs professional help.

Says his former pupil, Dr. Traisman:

"He wants to convince priests that it's not just a matter of seven Hail Marys."

To this end he is participating in the creation of a course in a project financed by the National Institute of Mental Health of the United States Public Health Service, designed to teach religious professionals about mental illness.

How well he will succeed in these aims is hard to predict. Despite the late Pope's expressed approval of psychiatry, there remains today great suspicion among American Catholics about psychiatry's purposes. The suspicion may well stem from ignorance; many Catholics still believe that psychiatry is a detour a sinner can take to avoid the consequences of his acts. Priests who know better deplore this tendency and feel that it is the result of the attack of a single man, Bishop Fulton J. Sheen. By virtue of his numerous TV appearances and his best-selling *Peace of Soul*, Bishop Sheen has come to stand for the Catholic viewpoint in the minds of many Americans, Catholic and non-Catholic alike. His attack on psychiatry, which he equates with communism, has been unrelenting for more than a decade.

But the current is running against Bishop Sheen, and support for the use of psychiatry to "assist" the Church continues to grow within the Church herself. And it could well be that the symbol that will ultimately win popular support for the cooperation of these two disciplines will be the man who has actually combined them in one person, Father Devlin. As one of his supporters put it:

"Just the fact that he exists is enough to make people wonder whether religion and psychiatry are contradictory."

EARL A. LOOMIS, Jr., M.D.

Earl Loomis grew up in a fundamentalist Baptist environment whose most prevalent, church-encouraged assumption was that "if you smoked a cigarette, you would inevitably drink, take a woman, and go straight thereafter to hell." Today, as the first psychiatrist ever to work full time at a theological seminary, he is hip deep in a movement that intends—as one of its aims—to expunge the hypocritical and neurotic from Protestant morality.

He works on the most intimate level possible with candidates for the ministry, hoping to make them understand the scientific as well as religious reasons why they and others act as they do—at times in seeming contradiction to the word of God. Because the seminary is Union, in New York, the most influential in Protestant thought in the United States today, Dr. Loomis, by indirection alone, could become one of the most significant figures in American religious and moral life.

Already he is so well regarded by fellow psychiatrists that many of them, queried on questions involving religion and psychiatry, suggest that you "see Loomis." As one renowned analyst put it: "If you want to know anything about that field, you talk to him."

So pronounced is this referral habit that one fully expects to meet an elderly, seasoned doctor. One finds, instead, a young man in his middle thirties who, because he wears a very close crew cut, looks even younger.

Dr. Loomis is chairman of the American Psychiatric Association's committee on religion and psychiatry, and this may explain some of the referrals. His unusual position at Union would explain others. But a good portion of his reputation is clearly due to his infectious enthusiasm for what he believes is the most important movement of our times.

Enthusiasm is a natural state for him. He is restless to a point that he walks faster than most people. He is intent to a point that not to watch his eyes when he speaks is to miss part of the conversation. They never leave you and they seem to sharpen in intensity as he makes his points. He is wildly metaphoric in his speech, but he is extraordinarily effective because no matter how much he mixes his figures, he is always talking about people.

"I'm a guy who wants things both ways," he explained once. "I'm not able to reject the other side of the dichotomy. I've got to embrace it, instead. I have a feeling that both psychiatry and religion can be related.

"Union Seminary is a place for me to see man's nature in a double image. Psychiatry has gotten very close to the nature of man, but religion knows a lot about man, too. The only trouble is, religion's asleep.

"Theology is like a great big library with untranslated, unrecognized treasures. What it knew of man got formalized; in seeking to preserve truth, theology put truth in the deep freeze. Now it's got to be thawed out.

"Theology became a struggle of ideas for the sake of ideas, rather than a channel of communication by which man may find enjoyment and fulfillment. It's like playing with dietary laws while people starve in the streets.

"Truth must come alive in terms of current human needs.

We've got to explore and experiment and see how religion can get hooked up to life."

This is a big order for a young man, but those who have seen his record do not question that Dr. Loomis is the man for the job. Before he was twenty-four, he had three college degrees, one his M.D., and he would have had them a year sooner had it not been for a year of study at Princeton Theological Seminary when he thought he wanted to be a minister. Although by 1958 he had been a doctor for only thirteen years, his résumé of internships, residencies, special post-graduate courses, training in psychiatry and psycho-analysis, teaching, private practice, service, licensure, hospital appointments, supervision experiences, memberships, service at theological seminaries, and publications, covered four crowded, single-spaced pages of elite type.

His specialty is child psychiatry, and one testimony to his competence was his being chosen, in 1955, as successor to Dr. Benjamin Spock as chief of the sections of child psychiatry and child development at Western Psychiatric Institute in Pittsburgh.

But the Pittsburgh appointment is also testimony to his sense of mission, because shortly after his appointment, when Union asked him to direct its program in psychiatry and religion, he unhesitatingly resigned the Pittsburgh job.

Acceptance of the Union offer meant the additional sacrifice of giving up a lucrative guaranteed income, and because Dr. Loomis supports eight people, only four of whom are immediate family, the decision was not a simple one. But, considering his own religious experience, the choice of Union was inevitable.

"My parents were fundamentalist Baptists of the Bible Belt variety—evangelistic, biblical literalists. They were both smart people—my father was an eye, ear, nose, and throat man—but they made religion a hell on earth for themselves.

"Yet religion was a very real point of strength in a very troubled home. My father was a man of unlimited generosity. You asked him for something and he'd say, 'How much?' There were three boys and one girl in the family, and there always seemed to be a number of shirttail relatives around the place. But my father had a lot of worry, a lot of family troubles, a lot of somatic illness. You might say that our home was more glorious and more hectic than most.

"I was a prude about religion. I used it much more than the average kid to solve my problems of adolescence. It was such a firm, unconditional thing with us that it sort of by-passed my sexual and vocational problems.

"This went on until I was fifteen. Then I hit the doctrine of hell. It really stunned me. I said, 'If this is what God's like, I don't believe in this. If God's this much of a devil, why should you do anything for Him?'

"So I studied the Bible by myself. In my own biased way I found the answers I needed to reject the possibility of eternal damnation. But I was still rigid and hyperreligious until the following year when I met a very impressive girl. She humanized me. By the time I got to college, I was a somewhat happy Puritan."

It was his study of psychiatry that finally brought Dr. Loomis to an understanding of the extreme variations in his religious life. He found out that, like many other people, he had not been taught an adequate conception of God.

"There are three categories of God we must deal with," he explains now. "The first is God as He really is—and this we can't ever know. The second is the ideal of God as taught in our churches, the true, pure, gentle, benevolent, loving God. The purest rendering of the religious message gives you this God.

"But there is a third category of God, and here's where

we run into trouble. At some point in his life an individual begins to develop a *private* notion of God. God is supreme; his father is supreme; therefore God must be like his father, only more so. If the father is rough, unkind, unpleasant, prohibitory, then what is God if not all these things?

"God thus becomes authority: eat this, do that, don't, don't, don't. God is like the ancient Hebrew God, Yahweh, a jealous God to be feared, a God to whom we must make sacrifice.

"If love of God means destruction of life, then we're in love with a Moloch."

His reference was to the Canaanite idol to whom children were sacrificed as burnt offerings in biblical times. While such sacrifices are unknown today, Dr. Loomis contends that there are uses to which God is put by unenlightened individuals that are virtually as dangerous.

"I can talk about the kind of images of God that get stuffed down kids' throats. I can talk of people who think of God in terms of 'Help me. I'm stuck,' or 'Kiss it and fix it.' I can talk about a patient who thinks God holds a bull whip."

To illustrate he tells the unpleasant story of a man who at forty-two was married, a father of three, and a chronic masturbater. A devout Catholic, he would run to confession after every act. But he could not find relief. Raging, he would rush home and beat his children, then repeat the cycle all over again.

One day Dr. Loomis asked him how he pictured God.

"God," said the man, "holds a bull whip."

"Here was a guy who had believed ever since he was a kid that God watched every wicked thing he did, and God would knock him dead.

"I was like that guy at one point," Dr. Loomis admits.

"To me the church was like the doctor who writes the pre-scription but doesn't get it filled.

"Analysis for me made my religion come alive. I've never been loved that way before—and yet the analyst never said, 'I love you.' He was in no sense beating the drums for theology, but just the experience of seeing what love could do by working with him made religion for me a relationship of love rather than fear.

"Now I know that God says to people, 'I don't delight in your burnt offerings. I'm with you only when you're in love.'"

Here, thinks Dr. Loomis, is the answer to critics who say that psychiatry can take away an individual's religion.

"When a person asks me, 'Will psychiatry take away my religion?' I say, 'I don't know. If your religion is a dead relic, yes. If it's something that's fulfilling sick needs, as those needs are modified and eliminated, religion will lose the purpose you are using it for. So you may lose religion. On the other hand, you may discover that there are great untapped re-sources in your religion that your illness kept you from seeing.'"

What Dr. Loomis himself wants to see realized is what he calls "a ministering" church, as contrasted with a church ministered to. In such a ministering church, parish members are emotionally equipped to give one another acceptance, love, and disciplined care.

"A congregation should not be a minister's hospital," he says. "It should be his corps of doctors."

The reason Dr. Loomis is at Union is that he feels many ministers today are not equipped to help their church be-come a ministering church. He believes that many ministers with churches as well as those who are just entering the ministry do not see themselves as they should. They have a

distorted idea of themselves "in role," and the distortion is
reflected in their view of people and their problems.

There are, he feels, three basic role distortions:

The priestly—"This guy thinks he's a mediator between
God and man. He's a sacramentalist. He wants to make the
divine and human meet on the level of some kind of professional religious magic. He thinks, 'A man is someone I can
lay my hands on and bless.' "

The prophet—"This is the kind of minister who figures
he more or less has the inside dope. If people get the word,
he figures they'll be fixed. He thinks, 'A man is someone
who's got to be told.' "

The first-aid man—"This is the jack-of-all-trades repair-
man. He can intervene and make things right. He's always
tearing all over the world fixing things. He forgets about
theology entirely. He thinks, 'A man is someone who is a
victim of circumstances that can be modified.' "

Each of these categories has a certain amount of validity.
But by itself each one is a caricature of a minister, says Dr.
Loomis.

It is the intention of Dr. Loomis's program at Union
to bring the potential minister to a "Gee, whiz" experience,
in which he sees the force of his office and its considerable
effect on people. The minister candidate is given certain
lifelike situations to act out, or "role play" with a make-
believe parishioner. Afterward he says, "Gee whiz, did I do
that to him?"

Seeing what he does to people as minister, and taking the
role of a parishioner himself at times, enables the candidate
to realize the difference between the "spectator-type" and an
encounter-type religious ministry.

"There's a kind of theology that's like a corpse," Dr.
Loomis insists. "A corpse can't talk back. You're not a doctor

until you see the difference between the corpse on the table
and the man who says, 'I hurt.' Nor are you a minister."

Earl Loomis would be the first man to acknowledge that
countless ministers were able to embody all of the best aspects of a man of God long before the new science of man
had a name. But he believes that the time is ripe in the
Protestant ranks for "hooking religion up to life" and he
feels the chances for this are better today than they have
been for two thousand years. He is firmly convinced that the
way to make the church dynamic is for the church to take the
best of what psychiatry has to give.

"How can I prove it?" he asks rhetorically. "By the next
twenty years of my life."

RABBI I. FRED HOLLANDER

To most people the figure of the Orthodox rabbi has been
to Judaism what the person of the priest has been to Christianity—the extreme of devotion, piety, and preoccupation
with theistic thought. More like the ascetic priest than his
parish counterpart, the best of the Orthodox rabbis has been
a scholar in a sense that has been largely lost to the Western
world. The material to which he gives his life in study, the
Talmud, is an exquisite interpretation of a history that
reaches 1,500 years before the birth of Jesus Christ. As if
this fact were not isolating enough, the prescriptions of piety
he fulfills in the form of costume and ritual are of the sort
to give him an appearance that, to modern eyes at least, seems
out of this world.

Now consider Fred Hollander. Young, urbane, with an
elegance to his manner, his voice is so measured that he
requires two seconds to say "hello" on the telephone, and
when he speaks in a room, the room takes on the feeling of

a cathedral. Yet when he is aroused, when he is speaking from conviction, he exhibits the passion of genius.

When he *is* in such a state, he is usually talking about psychiatry and religion. Like Father Devlin and Dr. Loomis, Rabbi Hollander sees religion, always volcanic in meaning, at last overflowing into life. Where before, his and other faiths had failed to arouse people, he feels they will now become involved with meaningful problems and restore themselves to the position of significance they deserve.

Fred Hollander was typical of most Orthodox American rabbis to a point. He studied the Talmud and related subjects at the center of American Orthodox Judaism, Yeshiva University in New York City. Ordained in 1946, he had achieved that same impressive mien of erudition that distinguishes so many good rabbis. But when his classmates went to positions in temples throughout the United States, Fred Hollander went to work at Bellevue Hospital in New York. Having drifted into counseling work at that enormous public institution during his student days, he now saw no reason to leave.

"It felt good to make people feel good," he explains simply.

In addition to working with patients, he began to train rabbinical students in pastoral counseling work. The demand for his services grew, and what had been at first an informal affair suddenly developed into a formal course. Today it attracts not only students from Yeshiva, but from Reformed Judaism's Hebrew Union College in New York as well.

Like Father Devlin and Dr. Loomis, Rabbi Hollander has a distinctive style of speech. His makes jarring contrasts of past and present. A perfect example is the manner in which he breaks his Bellevue course into three aspects:

1. Judaism's concept of man.
2. The behavioral sciences' concept of man.
3. What they mean to Mrs. Cohen.

Mrs. Cohen—or Miss or Mr. Cohen—is an important person in Rabbi Hollander's life. When he is talking about religion and psychiatry, she dominates his talk. She can be like the loquacious young woman he once saw in the hospital who had just lost a breast in surgery. Over and over again she described to the rabbi how her boy friends had always complimented her on her figure, and of how once it had even been compared to that of a famous actress. Now she felt she had been reduced to nothing.

Similarly, Mrs. Cohen can be like a woman in the hospital who had undergone a colostomy. To Rabbi Hollander she cried: "I'm no longer the woman my husband married."

"She is a person, breast or no breast, colostomy or no colostomy," the rabbi cries in turn. "The clergy must emphasize that every person is given the responsibility of recognizing that he is a somebody, simply because he is a creature of God."

But most of the time Mrs. Cohen is just Mrs. Cohen, an ordinary, well-meaning woman who is not sick, but who nonetheless has the common, mainly depressing problem of finding love and joy in a *mishuga* world. It is through this person's needs that Rabbi Hollander is able to find fault with both religion and psychiatry.

Rabbi Hollander feels that the real value of fusion is not in dealing with religious neurotics, although he is all for helping them. He agrees with Father Devlin that it is a good thing for a clergyman to be able to recognize neurotic symptoms in a parishioner so that he can refer the sick person to psychiatric assistance. "But," says Rabbi Hollander, "the average rabbi doesn't have to be told to refer; he knows he's not competent to deal with a sick man; you tell him to refer, he's insulted. What he wants to know is what is he going to do about the people he shouldn't refer. You give him a lecture and he says afterward, 'Look, that's fine, but what am I going to tell Mrs. Cohen?'

"We have 168,000,000 people who are not psychotics in this country. What about them? These people are normal enough to accept cosmic values if they are transmitted successfully. Give them a good religious orientation and their lives would be enriched. But you tell them to sit down and pray, you don't get anywhere. They have to know how to pray. They have to appreciate what prayer is. They don't know now.

"We want to teach religion to adolescents. An adolescent always sees things in extremes. Something is either great or it stinks. How do we teach them religion without their becoming bigots?

"The psychiatry of today is still oriented toward sickness. But what can it tell us about the kids? It hasn't told us anything yet. What can it tell us about how we can give something to the old people? Take away their mah jongg today and what have you got? We couldn't take it away—there wouldn't be anything left. But couldn't psychiatry give us something so that in thirty years religion would mean something besides mah jongg to old people?

"What can the clergy learn from psychiatry that will keep religion from being a long, lost weekend for a normal person? It's the normal people the clergy see."

Today, the rabbi insists, ordinary people are ready for insights that will give both religious and psychological validity to their lives. "People ten years ago didn't see the relevance of income to ulcers. Now they see it." And not only are people ready, he feels, but the language is ready; it can spell out these new ideas that can enrich life.

A good example is the manner in which a clergyman would treat the concept of "sacrifice." Says Rabbi Hollander:

"When we talk about sacrifice today, we can't talk about

giving something to some abstract concept. We have to say that by sacrifice you achieve completeness. Only in loving when you're threatened, when it hurts, when you don't want to love, can you get back the kind of love that makes *you* a complete and happy person."

The other side of the argument is that many rabbis today are not equipped to talk about sacrifice or most any other religious concept in terms that have meaning to Mrs. Cohen.

"Look through any number of books of old sermons," he challenges. "The relation of religion to life is simply not there. Not so long ago I delivered a sermon to four hundred rabbis in which I related the Bible to everyday problems— and to *them* it was a novelty.

"We have to rephrase the theology so that religious resources can be related to people in day-to-day living. Rabbis for too long have had a certain naïveté concerning insights. They've been too scholarly, too theistic. Now they must not only translate for people, they must *reach* people.

"What we want to do is make the clergyman aware of how important it is for him to have an idea of a man as a psychological being. Religion is his principal resource for helping people—no question about that. But we tell him that in order to help them he has got to become a bit of a psychologist."

That this emphasis is a major development in American Judaism today—Orthodox, Conservative, and Reformed— Rabbi Hollander has no doubt. As proof, he cites the fact that between 80 and 90 per cent of congregations seeking rabbis today "seek and prefer" what they call a "modern" rabbi.

"Religion today has little use for the exclusively pious rabbi," he feels. "Today Orthodox rabbis of the old school find it hard to survive. They say that people are not interested in piety. That isn't quite true. They want some piety, but they also want a rabbi who 'understands me.'"

The test of a religion's liveliness today is whether religious ideas can get all the way from the pulpit to Mrs. Cohen. Rabbi Hollander is encouraged to believe that the test is being passed.

"Religion," he says, "has taken all the concepts it's been preaching about for centuries without practical application —and finally put them in the kitchen."

4.

"JESUS LOVES ME, THIS I KNOW, MY PSYCHIATRIST TOLD ME SO"

A BEVERLY HILLS, CALIFORNIA, psychiatrist who was an ordained rabbi before he took up medicine tells the story of a Jew who was shipwrecked on a deserted island. To keep from losing his mind, he decided to build a city.

Using stones, driftwood, and other raw materials, he did. When, many years later, rescuers arrived to take him back to civilization he proudly insisted that they first make a tour of his project.

"That's my house over there," he told them, "and there's the temple. Down there's the grocery and the post office, and beyond that is the other temple . . ."

"The other temple?" a rescuer asked.

"Yes. That's the one I don't go to."

To the man who tells it this story illustrates a dynamic new understanding about people's beliefs in God. Says the psychiatrist, Emanuel M. Honig:

"Everyone's God is different."

Few authorities today would dispute the conclusion. For it is in this area of how individuals conceive of God and what they conceive Him to be that psychiatry has made what is possibly its most significant contribution to religion. As a result of psychiatry's revelations, the part of the individual in formulating religious ideas has been recognized as something that often exists apart—embarrassingly apart—from good theological concepts. People, it has been learned, not only constantly reinterpret the idea of God; they manipulate it in terms of their own problems or prejudices, serving themselves but staining the purity of religious ideals.

That the concept of God has been used idolatrously by certain elements of every religion at one time or another in history has been no secret even to religion. But today more and more clergy are insisting that psychiatry has not only illuminated for them the reasons for such idolatrous practices but has given religion the missing tools it has needed to extinguish flagrant religious distortions.

The distortions almost inevitably center on one notion— that God is a vengeance-wreaking old man who one day will knock the believer dead.

Recent observations have revealed this undesirable notion of God as one that is far more common than had ever been suspected. Some authorities now contend that the unwarranted concept is even more prevalent in the unconscious minds of religious people than the official and desirable concept of God as a loving, accepting, forgiving father.

The disclosures did not result from idle theorizing. Rather, they were drawn from data that made their discovery a grim one—case studies of individuals who had been unconsciously terrorized by the belief that God was after them, and who ultimately had had to seek psychiatric treatment for their difficulties. So frequently had this situation been encountered that among the initiated a few years ago it gave rise to a bitter parody on a well-known religious hymn that went:

> "Jesus loves me, this I know,
> My psychiatrist told me so."

But if the subject is material for jokes to some, it is a grim one for others. Many clergymen do not like to discuss it, first because it is subject to misinterpretation unless explored fully, and second because it cannot help but reflect adversely on certain elements of organized religion, and thus inadvertently on religion itself. On the same floor of one well-known Protestant seminary, for example, these responses were obtained from three well-known theologians:

First Minister: "There is a pharisaical element in the church today that is undergoing challenge and change. Twenty years ago many people thought of God as a person who does nothing but condemn and of whom they should be afraid. Is psychiatry changing their ideas about God? I record them by the dozen."

Second Minister: "Fully half the people in this country harbor a feeling that God is judgmental. The American man has a need for this God. That's what he's used to. That's what he's comfortable with. He insists on his God being a bastard."

Third Minister: "I've never known anyone who was afraid of God."

Which of these assessments was right? Are people really afraid of God? How do they come to conceive of God? What influence do historical patterns play? Do conceptions of God differ from century to century? And what influence, if any, has psychiatry played in the manner of interpreting God? These may very well be uncomfortable questions, but if answers are possible, an attempt should be made to find them.

Religious history is brutal, and anyone who denies this is simply denying fact. In the popular mind, and despite the protestation of biblical scholars, the Old Testament God of the ancient Hebrews, Yahweh, is an oppressive figure, terrifying in his omniscience, fearful to contemplate in his wrath. As to Christianity, the record of violence in its behalf has been chronicled many times, most thoroughly in recent years by Oscar Pfister, a noted psychiatrist, minister, and religious historian. His summary in *Christianity and Fear* [1] is unforgettable:

The monstrous volume of anti-Christianity discoverable in the history of Christianity ... which ought to unite men in competing for the realization of the love of Jesus ... in fact revealed innumerable instances of savage and uncharitable disputes about dogmas, sacraments, and ecclesiastical powers.

A history of Christianity, Pfister goes on:

showed how innumerable heretics were tortured and killed, allegedly in the name of Jesus, though in fact they, too, loved Christ and had drawn their ideal of Him from the Bible and from their conscience; how hundreds and thousands of witches were burned to death by men who thought themselves God's champion; and how murderous wars were waged with hate and savagery.

Religious history, Pfister notes, is laced with:

endless disputes on dogma conducted with a hate, fanaticism, and cruelty proportionate to the subtlety, incomprehensibility, and remoteness from the reality of love characterizing the trivialities with which they were concerned ... quivering anxiety about the individual's salvation when he found his conscience commanding him to diverge from ordinances of the Church; furious hatred of heretics ... compelled by their study of the Bible ... and practical experience ... to refuse adherence and belief to ecclesiastical dogma ...

[1] *Christianity and Fear,* translated by W. H. Johnston (New York: The Macmillan Co., 1948), p. 9.

... all these, I found, roused a much greater interest than the task of realizing Divine and human love.

But if it is true that religious history is replete with violence and oppression, it is equally true that both Judaism and Christianity are suffused with love. While most Christians today will tell you that forgiveness is a concept that originated with Christ, religious historians will contend otherwise. The forgiving God is amply represented in the Old Testament, according to Dr. Maurice S. Friedman, a philosopher-author-historian, who teaches at Sarah Lawrence College. Even the Talmud, the commentary on the Old Testament, is a document in which the merciful character of God is *inseparable* from His strict justice, despite the fact that in the minds of the Hebrews one quality, then the other, appears to prevail. So with Christianity do we find its adherents worshiping an uncompromising and even a fierce God in one century and a benevolent God in another.

There are many explanations for why the personality of God changes in the minds of people from time to time. Professor Herbert Wallace Schneider, a religious historian of Columbia University, believes that current events affect people's notions of God. In time of harmony and abundance, for example, people would tend to look upon God as gentle and less demanding, but in times of uncertainty, as in the last several decades, people would tend to be uncertain of God's whims. God, they would figure, was about as risky to deal with as the economy, or war and peace.

Many theologians cite man's control over his world as a significant factor in determining people's attitudes toward God. They point out that scientific mastery of the world has increased to a point where we all feel we can do something about most of the elemental problems that confront us. Science has created a situation in which we are almost certain we will not go hungry or be without clothing and shelter. Says Rabbi Jerome D. Folkman of Temple Israel in Columbus, Ohio: " 'Who is the mightiest man? He who has conquered himself.' Man is more in control now. Thus he fears God less."

Sociologists and anthropologists point out that there can be a cultural influence in theology. A favorite example in this category is the Irish, among whom a vengeful God concept is consistently more apparent than among other groups of Catholics.

Even such seemingly extraneous concepts as brotherhood and political philosophies that advance the idea of working together, such as our own democracy, can influence people's attitudes about God, a San Francisco psychiatrist, Dr. Carl Jonas, contends.

But the significant thread through all these arguments is that man, unable to know empirically who and what God is, actually arrives himself, on the basis of his experiences and the attitudes deriving therefrom, at his own God concept. God is an idea of man's. It cannot actually be proved by the people who believe; even they admit that God must be accepted on faith. Where psychiatry comes in is that, more than any other science, it has studied the manner in which man realizes ideas. It knows the factors that influence these ideas; it therefore might be expected to know something about how man comes to conceive of God.

As expected, it does. The "classical" explanation of how the idea of God develops in a child is no different from the one supplied by Dr. Earl Loomis:

At some point in his life, the child begins to develop a *private* notion of God, apart from mystical or church-taught notions. He has heard that God is supreme. But what is "supreme," if not something akin to his own father, who is the most supreme thing the child has ever known? The child then decides that God must be like his father, only more so. What is his own father like? Isn't he the man who makes you do all the things you don't want to do? Then God must make you do what is even worse.

Complicating the problem is the use to which many parents have put God in the home. Far more prevalent than a discussion of God's love, according to many clergymen and psychiatrists alike, is the use of God as a policeman.

"God has been the disciplinarian person for parents," says Dr. Maurice A. Riseling, a minister and now a clinical psychologist in Santa Ana, California. "Children as a result identify with the devil, who has all the fun. God they hate."

This seems like a pretty juvenile concept of religion. It is. But if the psychiatrists are right, *it is also the concept with which most of us approach religion all through life.*

Religiously, in other words, we seldom grow up. Most Americans attend regular schools for at least twelve years, and an increasing number go on to college and graduate studies. But few of them ever get beyond the sixth grade of Sunday school and, until recently at least, many of those who did had been subjected to unenlightened instruction by untrained personnel. A revolution in Sunday-school methods and curriculum, which will be described farther on, is testimony to the importance religious groups attach to discoveries that adults have been hobbled all their lives by infantile notions of God. For many authorities now contend that most religious people, while outwardly promoting and projecting the love of God, forever remain unconsciously afraid of His wrath. In psychiatric terms, they never come to terms with "authority figures." Many psychiatrists and psychologically oriented clergymen place the number of people in this category well above 50 per cent. A few estimates go as high as 80 and 90 per cent.

Whether resolved or not, the problem must at some point

be faced by everyone, even by professed agnostics, some psychiatrists now contend. One who does is Dr. Joseph Wheelwright of San Francisco. Since he is a Jungian analyst, his
evaluation is particularly significant, because the Jungians,
the first group to make a major break with Freud, see man's
orientation as *religious* rather than sexual.

Dr. Wheelwright made these observations:

"Even if people consider themselves agnostic, nonetheless
there is a very potent God image somewhere down in the
unconscious. It is obvious that an individual discovering
the image will react with the sort of awe that is induced by
witnessing a thunderstorm, a tempest, or childbirth. An unknown force of great potency always induces fear."

That this image exists in all of us can be seen, Dr. Wheelwright feels, by the fact that when anyone undergoes depth
therapy the image surfaces.

"After a certain amount of analysis this image tends to
become activated, jazzed up. At this point its nature has to
be explored. How much is inherent? How much was put
there? The individual has to come to terms with what he
finds."

In the light of current events, Dr. Wheelwright's next
remark seems particularly significant.

"The tendency in analysis is to sweeten the parental image
and to encourage the permissive aspect of the parental figure
and thus God."

This statement mirrors precisely what is going on in many
religious circles today.

There is an increasing acceptance of the idea that people
do get their notion of God from their relationship to some
human figure. "It isn't adequate to describe God and present
Him to children," says Dr. Jonas of San Francisco, a Catholic.
"It's the God substitutes, the parents, who determine the
attitude children will have about God. The priest has some

influence, but it is subordinate to the relationship the person has had with his own parents."

Many psychiatrists would agree completely with Dr. Jonas's estimate. A few would disagree; they feel that in adult life the clergyman is at least as powerful an influence as were parents in childhood. Dr. Honig, once a full-time rabbi who still teaches at seminaries and conducts High Holy Day services, thinks the clergyman is an even more potent father figure than the parent.

In either case, there is a tendency to soften up on what the clergy have to say about God. A Presbyterian minister, Joseph Bishop of Swarthmore, Pennsylvania, contends: "I can spot a guy who's had psychiatric orientation in the first ten sentences of his sermon. The emphasis is whole. A man who's been oriented cannot preach a sermon about the judgment of God without reference to the love of God. He has seen the ravaging effects of an exclusive emphasis on the judgment of God."

Mr. Bishop cites himself as his own best example. He recalls preaching a sermon several years ago on the eternal destiny of the human soul, in which he said that some souls were so removed from spiritual reality that all God could do was to "cut them off." After the sermon, a young woman came to see him. She was terrified. Questioning her, he learned that she was a compulsive liar. His sermon had convinced her she was doomed. Said Mr. Bishop: "After I saw the suffering I had caused her, I was never again able to preach a sermon like that."

At Loyola University of Chicago, where the government-sponsored course in mental health for priest candidates is being created, Father Vincent V. Herr, a psychologist and colleague of Father Devlin, notes that priests often in the past used to stress the fear motive "when nothing else would work."

"This practice has been exaggerated by people who didn't know how dangerous it was. We know now it's not effective; it sometimes leads to complexes, obsessions, and guilt feelings. In other words, hell, fire, and brimstone doesn't work. We're going to put that in our course."

The "complexes, obsessions, and guilt feelings" induced by an improper fear of God form a significant body of psychiatric case histories that are drawn from all three major faiths. Significantly, in almost every case where a cure was achieved, the therapy involved a recovery of the idea that God loved the individual and was not intent on striking him down.

One such transformation occurred in Columbus, Ohio, several years ago in a woman who had been making life miserable for herself, her husband, and their three children. She was unbearably jealous of the children, and could not stand to have her husband show them affection. A psychiatrist treating her isolated the reason: she had never had enough love from her own father, and unconsciously wanted her husband to be a father substitute. Knowing of the woman's religious background, the psychiatrist called the Reverend Roy A. Burkhart of the First Community Church in Columbus. After describing the case, he warned the minister: "She'll call you when you won't want to see her."

Late one Saturday night she called the minister. He told her he would see her right away.

"I hate God," she began at once.

"Tell Him," said the minister.

"How do you talk to Him?"

"Talk to Him the way He talks to you," Mr. Burkhart said. He recalls what followed.

"So she cursed God. She called God a son of a bitch. And suddenly she smiled. She said to me, 'In the very act of cussing Him out I knew peace.' "

At this point she finally told her story. Her parents had been missionaries in the Far East; her father had been captured by the Japanese, and had died in a prison camp. It was the woman's belief that because God had deprived her of her father, He must therefore hate her.

"Once I knew that she thought God hated her I could help her," Mr. Burkhart said.

Psychiatrist Loomis's patient, whose God held a bull whip, is another example. This man, it will be remembered, was a forty-two-year-old father of three who was overcome by a problem of masturbation. A Catholic, he would confess his sins, but could not find relief from his guilt.

"The only way this man could be made healthy was if he could convince himself that God was accepting and forgiving," Dr. Loomis concluded.

One day, in the midst of cursing Loomis, the man broke off. "Wait a minute," he said. "I'm swearing at you and you're not telling me I can't. You're not punishing me."

"That was the break-through," Dr. Loomis recalls. "In analysis I had become a father figure for him. When he realized that his father figure could be kind and forgiving, God could suddenly be kind and forgiving. He in turn could be kind to his children. His theology and personal problems both straightened out."

Often a theological adjustment becomes a key to physical recovery. The Reverend Paul E. Johnson, professor of psychology of religion and director of the pastoral counseling service at Boston University School of Theology, has written of one man who suffered for years with an ulcerated colon. A psychiatrist had helped him discover that his basic problem was hatred toward his father and that he was also engaged in a combat with God. When he found himself accepted by a pastoral counselor who had come to stand for his father and his God, he began to find his cure.

In recounting the experience later, the young man had a dramatic exchange with members of Dr. Johnson's staff.

JOEL: "I have said that we could sum up the experience here in one word of four letters, spelled L-O-V-E, and for the first time in my life I have felt its impact. I have never felt that here I was a burden, unwanted, impossible, a dumb dodo, nothing like that. In fact, I sometimes felt insecure because somebody didn't lay the whip on me. . . . "

COUNSELOR I: "It seems to me we arrived at some conclusion that your inability to establish or continue a relationship with your father who died had prompted your physical difficulty; and from then on you began to improve physically. . . . That to my mind was the turning point."

JOEL: "That is correct. By December there was a marked decrease in the hemorrhaging and by the following November, when my family doctor examined me, he said it was wonderful; he had never seen anything like it. . . . "

STAFF I: "At one time did you feel God was against you?"

JOEL: "I felt that until I came here. I mean I never wanted to believe that God really cared. . . . "

STAFF I: "Has your feeling toward God changed in these experiences?"

JOEL: "Definitely, yes. . . . It was at about this same time that my counselor began to get to me with the idea that God is a forgiving Father, always ready to accept us, but that for Him to make Himself felt we must forgive ourselves even as He forgives us." [2]

A somewhat similar case occurred in Columbus with Rabbi Folkman. He visited a girl in the hospital who was suffering from a case of anorexia nervosa—starving herself to death. Her response to his presence was to vomit at the rabbi. When she calmed down, she told him she was two months pregnant but did not want her child. She and her

[2] *Religion in Life*, XXV (spring, 1956, New York: Abingdon Press), pp. 203-4. Copyright, 1955, by Pierce & Washabaugh.

husband had one child already which because of complica-
tions had cost them $3,000. The husband, a schoolteacher,
was not making much more than $4,000.

As Rabbi Folkman gained the girl's confidence, she spoke
more freely of her past. "I did things a girl shouldn't do,"
she told him. "I'm damaged goods."

Rabbi Folkman found out that the girl had been attacked
by a neighbor boy at the age of eleven. Since then she had
constantly felt guilty, expressing her guilt at times in over-
eating and later in promiscuity.

Rabbi Folkman said to her, "Don't you think you have
punished yourself enough already? God will forgive you."

But the girl would not believe that God forgives. "How
do you know?" she demanded.

"I told her this was a basic assumption of Judaism. In the
name of the Ten Commandments and of God, I forgave her,"
Rabbi Folkman recalls. To his joy, the girl asked him to
hand her a bottle of pop that had been standing, untouched,
on her night stand.

In another case a Los Angeles woman complained to her
doctor of a pain over her eye. Medical tests showed no physical defect. In treatment it developed that the woman, who
was unmarried, had been having relations with men from
time to time. Earlier she had given up Protestantism because she had been told that God observed all of man's
conduct. Now she was so guilt ridden that she couldn't
pray. "Her sore eye was merely a symptom of the eyesore
she thought she was to God," the psychiatrist, Dr. Honig
of Beverly Hills, relates.

Another Honig patient was a Catholic youth whose concept of God was a completely literalistic one—that He punished not only for doing but for thinking as well. The young
man had been promiscuous, and when he came to Dr.
Honig he was on the verge of a breakdown. His first hour he

did nothing but pace up and down the office. As in other cases, Dr. Honig's approach was to help the man re-evaluate his faith—and the doctor's greatest contribution in this regard was to accept the man's actions, without judgment, as clues to his real disturbance. One day, after several months of therapy, the man cried, "What type of God would it be who did not understand human foibles? How can God be divine if He cannot understand me?" The patient was soon able to stop treatment and return to his faith.

"None of us escapes our struggle with authority figures," Dr. Johnson of Boston University states. "Psychology helps us to see what the struggle is. The struggle itself may change one's theology from a stern God of wrath to a God who forgives and loves you."

Dr. Johnson then made a statement that in the same or similar words is one of the most frequently expressed views of clergymen who have used psychiatric findings to illumine their ministries.

"This is not a new theology. It's an old theology that was obscured due to the distortions of Puritanism and hell-fire and damnation. Religion today is rediscovering a living relationship to the God who forgives and restores the broken-hearted who seek Him."

It cannot be stressed too much that what is happening is happening neither everywhere nor to the same degree everywhere it is happening. There are in the American religious movements—particularly those grown from Puritan roots—tremendous gradations of belief and sophistication. No one has ever had to tell the enlightened theologian that "to err is human, to forgive, divine." Yet across town from where this benevolent parson holds forth may be another minister of the very same denomination who over the years has convinced his parishioners that they are wicked sinners who will surely be struck down by God's wrath.

Thus, while the problem today is infinitely more civilized than in the days of the Crusades, its basic ingredient remains identical to the cause of religious persecution. It is the reason why the man built two temples: God is different for different people, and because every individual wants the security of believing that his is the right belief, he wants everyone else to accept his God.

Such a condition, as the above cases clearly indicate, is one reason why formal religion can be a threat to its members. Notes Psychiatrist Gotthard Booth of New York City, who has been both active and eminent in the field of religion and psychiatry for years:

"The dogmatic specificity of a denomination may be so incompatible with the personality of a particular member that he cannot accept the Christian method under this form. He may therefore reject religion altogether, or he may find it a source of anxiety, not of strength." [3]

The difference between clergymen in the same faith may be accounted for by something so basic and obvious as their seminary training. The intellectual levels of seminaries in the United States are just as inconsistent as those of universities. Some are excellent. Some are terrible. Some jolt their students out of childish notions of God as a first step in training. Some never do, but, rather, buttress these unfortunate and immature attitudes.

"Any responsible seminary challenges childhood religion," Dr. Loomis of Union contends. "The seminary professors were shattering the illusions about God long before Freud. What psychiatry did was to enable the seminaries to *show* their students how and why they conceptualized God the way they did, and why their notions were inadequate."

One final, and most important, observation must be made.

[3] *The Church and Mental Health,* p. 17.

Every competent source agrees that while "sweetening up," as Psychiatrist Joseph Wheelwright put it, the parental and clerical figures and thus the figure of God can be a most constructive step when it occurs in the areas where it is needed, this is the precise point at which the clergymen involved can make their worst error—with untold injury to their parishioners. As Psychiatrist Frederick Hacker of Beverly Hills, California, points out, while psychiatry has unquestionably caused an enlightenment in certain fundamentalist groups of American religion by teaching them about the problems too much authority creates for people, there are nonetheless different forms of authority. Some of them are not only good, they are essential to an ethical existence. Says Dr. Hacker: "A man who would not recognize the authority of Einstein on matters of relativity is an idiot. And if there is a surgeon in a room of 100 people and someone is stricken with appendicitis, no one in his right mind is going to argue as to who should handle the case."

We do not question the authority of a parent when he forbids a child to cross the street. To fear a drunken driver is to be properly afraid. So, too, it seems patent, we must have concern for the need to live in accommodation with other human beings. In any society there are consequences for our acts. There is a form of authority that supports this sensible conclusion.

There is concern, therefore, that clergymen in their zeal will make the same mistake today that some parents made twenty years ago with permissive theories of child rearing. They went overboard, and the result in too many cases was a type of wilderness child who, never having heard the word "no," concluded that nobody cared about him. Feeling unloved, he created an atrocious record merely to call attention to himself.

Says Psychiatrist Carl Jonas of San Francisco:

"Understanding and acceptance are personality traits so desirable you can't have too much of them. But acceptance and understanding don't do away with the need for limiting, restricting, and prohibiting. There must be a place for the attribute of 'Thou shalt not.'"

A rabbi in the same city, Alvin Fine of Temple Emanuel, puts it this way: "I'm here to help and not to judge. But some authority is necessary. Some will must prevail."

The very men who cheer those of their colleagues who are fleeing today from a God of wrath also express concern that they will move too far and fast. They point out that a notion of God as being exclusively benevolent can undermine the moral strength of individuals. They cringe at songs that cry "Somebody up there likes me, right or wrong, good or bad." People who lean on notions of this sort fail to develop fully. As judicious clergymen point out, there are "inescapable aspects of God's demands for righteousness." Moreover, the very essence of love may be altered and even made meaningless by excessive permissiveness. Says Philosopher Maurice Friedman: "Not to understand that a demand may be part of God's love for man is to misunderstand love as meaning unconditional acceptance without demand, and to sentimentalize love, emptying it of any real content."

With the above qualification in mind, then, these central facts remain:

While some religious groups in the United States have balanced the judgment of God with His love, many others have not.

Among the groups that have not, there has been a significant movement in the last two decades from an exclusive emphasis on God's wrath toward a stress on God's love.

While many factors may have been involved in this striking shift, the most significant factor, in the judgment of the people involved, has been the findings of psychiatry.

Clergymen who now admit that they had in the past erroneously stressed God's wrath feel they have finally isolated the reason why religion has not been so effective as it might have been. They insist that religion would have sold itself to more people, and done more for those who did believe, had the whole element of authority, of God as a policeman, been sooner and better understood—and consistently tempered by stress on God's love.

"People generally dislike to do anything when there's a sense of oughtness to it," Rabbi Fred Hollander observes. "At least now we have a key. A key is very important."

5.

SIN OR SYMPTOM?

G OOD LORD," the New York City minister thundered from deep in his leather chair, "twenty years ago the average minister wouldn't even discuss homosexuality."

Said a California clergyman, his back to an office window that framed a lovely palm tree:

"What may have been sin when I was a boy we would now consider an illness that the man had no responsibility for. I used to think that any drunkard was a sinner. I know better now."

An Ohio minister, driving through his city's traffic en route to a hospital call, observed:

"People used to be made to feel that to be angry was to sin. The fact is that Job wasn't patient at all. In the traditional churches there is still a movement to repress emotions. But in the psychological churches there's a move to bring emotions, like anger, out in the open.

"When I first came to the church there was a terrific resistance by people who just wanted to be assigned to hell. The wrath of God and eternal punishment were being held out. Today there's a movement toward the transcendence of guilt." He meant in the same church.

"Sin?" said the Chicago chaplain, smiling. "We've muddled that question up good."

In these four comments is reflected a changing attitude toward sin that is slowly taking shape in three different forms among an increasing number of United States religious groups.

First, actions once denounced as sins are now accepted as "symptoms." In many churches today adultery is the same sin it was twenty years ago; the adulterer, however, may not necessarily be condemned. Blasphemy may be just as outrageous to the religious today as it ever was, but the man who takes the Lord's name in vain may not necessarily be assigned to hell. More and more frequently the question is being asked, "Is this man wicked, or is he sick?"

"For centuries," states the Reverend Otis Rice, a minister and chaplain for more than thirty years, and one of the significant pioneers of the pastoral counseling movement, "man was either a sinner or crazy. Today both psychiatry and religion ask what his sin, so called, means. He may be a sinner, officially, but that's secondary to the problem of why he's sinning."

The second significant change has been within a more fundamentalist element of the United States religious scene. Hundreds of clergymen who had once sought to govern the activities of their congregants are now refraining from the judgment of secular matters whose connection to religion has always been dubious. "Secular religion," the moralistic, prohibitory creeds created by individual clergymen or sects without theological justification, is in many instances on the wane.

These first two changing views of sin tend to be found most frequently within the Protestant movement, although in both cases there are overtones within Catholic and Jewish groups as well. The third, and most arresting, change in attitudes toward sin is found almost exclusively at the progressive end of the Protestant dimension. Key religious thinkers in this group, impressed with the emotional problems they feel result when religious standards are placed beyond what they consider the reach of human capacities, are now asking what right religion has to set these standards in the first place.

The results have been astounding. The negative position toward sexuality exhibited in many churches for many years is being slowly but steadily replaced by one holding that sensual pleasure is a gift of God, and that the Bible proves it. Reacting to this mood, certain ministers are privately— and in a few cases publicly—condoning conduct that generations of Americans have been conditioned to regard as sinful. Masturbation, for example, is seen as a normal stage in development that should cause no more concern on the part of parents than thumb-sucking or nail biting. It does no physical harm; its only danger is the guilt that attaches to it through popular misunderstanding of the religious position toward the act. Various forms of love play practiced by many people in spite of church censure are in certain instances now being viewed as natural expressions of love, perfectly acceptable so long as they are found agreeable to the lovers. Sexual deviation is being viewed with infinitely more tolerance. Finally, and most impressively, premarital intercourse is now seen in a radically different light in some religious circles than it has been before.

What elements produced this mood? What caused this penetrating self-analysis by many significant Protestant theologians? What caused the question of "sin or symptom?" to be raised by elements of all three faiths as a key determinant in fixing responsibility for one's acts? What caused

so many fundamentalist clergymen to narrow the focus of
their moral concern?

The subsidiary elements involved in these changes are
several, not the least of which, many clergymen now frankly
admit with a remarkable lack of self-charity, has been
competition. Books, magazines, and even to a certain extent
television and the movies are increasingly reflecting the
enlightenment of our times. Full clinical explanations for
the actions of characters, stated in unblinking language
that plainly gets the point across, are a commonplace. In
such an environment people who can obtain vital information
everywhere but in their churches are obviously going to lose
patience with their churches. Many clergymen will now
contend that there was a long period of Victorian and post-
Victorian immobility within many religious groups, in which
they simply refused to acknowledge the existence of sex.
Some critics are even blaming this lack of willingness to deal
frankly with people as a chief cause of the welter of religious
skepticism that has been a distinguishing part of the country's
personality in the last several decades.

While some churches have always been "hooked up to
life," as Dr. Earl Loomis of Union Seminary puts it, others
have not, and it is to this condition that many of our best
religious writers are addressing themselves today. Notes Dr.
Seward Hiltner of the Federated Theological Faculty of the
University of Chicago, a prominent figure in the pastoral
counseling movement:

We emerged not long since from an era in which, especially in
Anglo-Saxon lands, serious public discussion of sex was taboo.
That this was poor policy, and without biblical precedent, we
now know. From the Christian point of view it is of positive significance that such taboos and euphemisms have been broken
through.... Having facts about sex behavior, and consequent
insight into existing sex attitudes, there is no possible retreat

into an ostrichlike position. It has never been enough to say that
sex is taken care of by marriage. The Christian view of sex has to
do more than that. For good or for ill, the lid is off . . . [1]

The title of Dr. Hiltner's book, *Sex Ethics and the Kinsey
Reports,* identifies one of the elements he feels was responsible for lifting the lid. Another writer, William Graham
Cole, chairman of the Department of Religion at Williams
College, cites two further factors in a superb study, *Sex in
Christianity and Psychoanalysis.*[2] These are the sexual emancipation of women, by which even "good" women have
earned the right to enjoy erotic pleasure, and, growing out
of the first, the decline of the double standard of sexual
morality. Where a few decades ago sexual experimentation
before marriage was the "right" of men alone, today
most young women also have some form of experience prior
to marriage, Mr. Cole points out. "In such a time as this,"
he suggests, ". . . it seems to many that the religious elements
of society stand as the guardians of the sexual bastille."

This self-incriminating mood, one of the least advertised
yet most interesting features of Protestant religious thinking
in the last thirty years, has produced a volume of memorable
scholarship the quintessence of which is to be found in
Mr. Cole's lengthy study. On the basis of this research, he
makes this striking conclusion: "The Church has been guilty
of preserving and preaching a point of view not generic to
Christian faith, an attitude . . . which is not only unbiblical
but also anti-biblical. . . ."

But whatever group of elements is cited by interpreters
of the American religious scene, one of them inevitably
seems to stand out not only as the most significant, but as
the one that gave form to the others. In the final analysis,

[1] *Sex Ethics and the Kinsey Report* (New York: Association Press, 1953),
p. 84.
[2] New York: Oxford University Press, 1955, p. 285.

the destruction of certain attitudes toward sin was caused
by a fire started when the two old enemies, psychiatry and
religion, were rubbed together. As John Knox Jessup noted,
in behalf of the editors of *Life* in the magazine's imposing
special issue on Christianity in December 1955:

A generation or two ago American Christianity, both in its
Puritan and Catholic traditions, tended to account unclean the
animal aspects of the human body. Few attitudes have changed
so radically in the twentieth century. Depth psychology ... has
liberated one animal impulse after another from the cage of
Victorian taboo morality.`

Certainly countless churches did not require a concept
of the unconscious to understand that drinking, smoking, and
dancing, if considered religious sins, were enough to cast
millions of drinkers, smokers, and dancers into moral despair.
But many churches and their ministers apparently did need
some dramatic proof that their concern was misplaced. On a
more challenging level, the same problem is being raised
today in the area of sexual mores. The question raised:
If so many people do what the churches say they shall not,
as has been proved, is not the Church, in a sense, on the
side of illness rather than health? To many theologians
it was a humbling discovery that religious people who did
anyway what their church taught them not to do were frequently overcome by guilt and became emotionally ill.

It is this discovery—that neurotic problems are an inevitable
by-product of condemnatory religion—that has been one of
the strong unifying links of psychiatry and religion. It is
worth repeating, however, that the three major faiths have
not all been similarly affected, principally because all do not
start from the same situation.

To the Catholic, standards of sin are a fixed matter
established by divine law. "There is no middle between sin

and not sin," Father Vincent V. Herr of Loyola University in Chicago summarizes crisply. "The priests have certain minimum requirements that never change."

A statement of Rabbi Robert Katz, coordinator of the human-relations department of Hebrew Union College in Cincinnati, could stand as an able summary of the Jewish viewpoint toward psychiatry's contribution to morality. "We now know more about human motivations, know why people sin, know why they resist repenting or change. . . . While we may be less punitive in confronting the individual sinner, we still hold that there are objective moral standards by which individual, sinful acts will be measured."

What Rabbi Katz calls "objective moral standards" the Protestants in many cases describe as the "moral imperative." This is a term that would be defined differently by each of the sects but that essentially means the command to men to live together in a relationship of love, acceptance, and understanding. This imperative makes certain rather obvious demands on men. To put it bluntly, a man is not going to get along very well with his neighbor if he is having an affair with his neighbor's wife.

The conflict, if any, arises for all three faiths whenever human error creates a separation between individual interpretations of religious morality and what each faith holds to be the true biblical morality. It is a Protestant group that is now confronting this conflict. Jews and Catholics, in the main, are not confronting it, because for one reason or another they feel it doesn't exist.

But all three developments in the consideration of sin, regardless of how they are shared by the three faiths, do raise at least one provocative problem for any theological interpretation of man's role in the universe. It is the problem, mentioned earlier in the discussion of Father

Devlin, of how good we can be, even when we want to be good.

Notes one well-placed minister:

"Most of us have experienced occasions when, despite our efforts for self-control, we become overwhelmed by surges of deep emotional power which capture our defenses and make us helpless. Moral accountability should normally be expected from those who have the capacity to control their moral behavior, but one can hardly be held responsible for unconscious behavior which one is powerless to control. Traditional theology, free will, and cultural concepts of moral responsibility may need to be examined in the light of new research concerning the dynamics of the unconscious. Religion may be on the verge of developments as revolutionary as the Protestant Reformation."

That statement was written not by a great religious thinker but by an organizer. He is George Christian Anderson, an Episcopal minister and for many years a hospital chaplain. In 1954 Mr. Anderson incorporated an organization he called the National Academy of Religion and Mental Health. He rented a small office in a corner of the fourth floor of the Academy of Medicine on 103d Street and Fifth Avenue in New York City.

The response was incredible. As a clearinghouse for ideas of religiously oriented psychiatrists and psychiatrically oriented religionists, Mr. Anderson's organization grew so precipitously within a few years that it was able to plan a move into its own large quarters in a suburb of Philadelphia. And because of the composition of the response, the Academy had to drop the designation "national" from its name. It had, in four years, become world wide.

Although Mr. Anderson is the first to acknowledge that he is an organizer and not a philosopher, he is nonetheless an extremely sensitive man on whom the need for delicacy by one suspended between two wary, conglomerate groups would not be lost. For practical considerations alone, what he says about the implication for religion of psychiatric insights would surely reflect the clusters of attitudes with which he must deal; his own thoughts, therefore, can be read as reliably as a barometer.

Only rarely today does the barometer read "storm." The needle has moved slowly but deliberately away from the turbulence of hell-fire and brimstone toward the calm winds of grace. Ministers who had thought of right and wrong in terms of strict rules now think in terms of the individual and the specific problems that have made him do what he's done.

"The harsh spirit of the moralists has been yielding to a redemptive approach," explains the Reverend Paul E. Johnson of Boston University School of Theology. In other words, many clergymen who weren't before are now as concerned about saving the sinner as they are with condemning the sin. As a consequence of what they are learning about people from psychiatry, they have found that there are times when they can't do both—at least in the presence of the sinner.

An incident that dramatically conveys this idea of how significantly the approach of some members of the clergy to human conduct has changed is told by the Reverend Ernest E. Bruder, a chaplain at the United States Government hospital for the mentally ill, St. Elizabeth's, in Washington, D.C. Mr. Bruder has trained hundreds of young ministers in pastoral counseling techniques, and enjoys enormous respect among doctors and clergy alike. This is the story he told:

A minister had as a parishioner a girl who had lived with a married man for several years and at one point had borne him a child. The man and woman were very much in love, but the man could not get a divorce. Yielding to temptation, he had left his wife one day to find happiness with the girl he loved.

The girl, however, was weighted by tremendous guilt feelings. She had been, and still was, devout. She wanted her child baptized.

At this point she went to her minister. But the minister turned her away.

Later the minister experienced some guilt feelings of his own. He took his problem to the hospital chaplain under whom he had been studying depth psychology. The chaplain convinced him that he should baptize the child, thereby saving her religiously and her mother psychologically.

Another case was that of the woman "who had been to bed with men in three different cities." She went for help to a Washington, D.C., clergyman. She told him she was worried not that she had sinned against God—"oh, God will forgive me"—but that her friends would find out and disapprove. Here was a double challenge for the minister. For one thing, the woman had seemingly no respect for the requirements her God made upon people to live a moral life. Second, her acts had been against the moral precepts of the church.

It is a principle of psychiatry that a troubled person expressing a strong conviction, or acting overtly, is frequently covering up his true nature, which is exactly the opposite. Thus a child who is unconsciously terrified that he will lose his parents' love might take all sorts of chances in traffic to convince himself that he is afraid of nothing whatsoever. In the case of the woman, she did not believe that God would forgive her at all. She really thought religion boiled down to the scary idea that "Grandfather is watching you." Nor did she enjoy her promiscuous affairs. She indulged, it developed, because years before her brother had gotten into trouble, and her family had thereupon in-

sisted that she would have to be the example of virtue for the
entire family. Without realizing it, she had rebelled against
carrying this load of virtue.

Clearly, her subsequent actions were, in the church sense,
"sins." But had they been damned, and dropped at that,
she would never have learned why she was being promiscuous
—what she was covering up for—and would have gone on in
the same unhappy fashion. As it developed, when she understood why she was doing what she was, she stopped.

Thus far we have been discussing sins that remain sins,
even though their exculpation is handled differently than it
used to be. Now let us turn to two ways in which the categories of sin themselves are undergoing analysis and change.
The first of these occurs in a fundamentalist vein, where
actions that were once considered sins are simply not seen
in this sense any more. Numbers of clergymen, ruthlessly
self-critical, make revealing comparisons to illustrate how they
and their parishioners had been playing theology by ear,
and have come now to a more mature outlook toward human
habits. "It used to be that 'anything that gives you pleasure
is evil,' " the Reverend Otis R. Rice of New York comments.
"Sex was hush hush when I was a boy," remarked the Reverend W. R. Hall, a Southern California minister. "Not long
ago we had a girl who felt that if a man touched her she'd be
pregnant. We had her home and Mrs. Hall and I disabused
her of that before she left the house."

"Religion," says Maurice A. Riseling, of Santa Ana, California, a minister and now a practicing psychologist, "has
too long been concerned with the question of 'Is it good
or is it bad?' instead of 'Is it healthy or is it unhealthy?'
Alcohol was once a question of right or wrong. It is now
a health problem."

Many parishioners and clergymen who had always considered certain forms of conduct sinful, period, are baffled about

what to think now. As an illustration, the Reverend Dr. Rice was invited a few years ago to speak at a southern seminary. After his speech he was accosted on the platform by an agitated contingent of his audience. One of them spoke the question for all: "You didn't once mention a thing about drinking and smoking. Is this religion?" When Dr. Rice told him it was, the student responded, "You mean God is like this?"

While this incident may seem almost parochial to any sophisticated churchgoer, it must be remembered here, as well as with considerations of concepts of God, that there is wide variance, even within the same sect, of practices and beliefs. Recall, for a moment, the statement of Mills College's Dr. George T. Hedley. "It was a new experience for me when I came to this country that drinking, smoking, and dancing were religious issues. Religion in America is really much more strict, more puritanical than elsewhere."

Mr. Hedley is a Methodist minister. Yet the official position of the Methodist Church is one that most emphatically disapproves any use whatsoever of alcoholic beverages. "We have greatly intensified our emphasis upon total abstinence, as will be obvious from this year's Commitment theme, 'Drinking Is a Moral Issue,' " Dr. Caradine R. Hooton, general secretary of the Methodist Board of Temperance, noted in a 1958 letter. "We insist that for Christians temperance is a moderate or modest use of things helpful and abstinence from things hurtful. We think that any use of alcoholic beverages is harmful."

Dr. Hooton's observations officially discredited reports I had heard that the Methodists were changing their stand on liquor from total abstinence to temperance. But an incident that occurred a few weeks after the reports leads me to wonder whether these intuitive evaluations were far from what is beginning to happen in some individual Methodist groups. In gathering material, I had set my schedule so that I might spend a Sunday in my wife's home town, San Pedro, California, where several years before we had attended an Easter service in the Methodist church where she had received her religious education. I well remembered how on that day of rejoicing the presiding minister, a big, friendly, passionate man, had stood before the banks of lilies and cried to his congregation that liquor was the brew of the devil, and drinking led to hell. It seemed to me that if there were any changes in what individual Methodist ministers were saying about liquor as a sin, here was a good way to find out.

I found that the old minister had retired. The new man, much less given to dramatics, spoke that day—and incidentally to a full house, despite some glorious weather outside— about the Los Angeles divorce rate, which happens to approximate the number of marriages. He did mention liquor— but as one of several outlets sought by emotionally disturbed people whose homes are breaking up. He never once mentioned drinking as a "sin," or suggested that the use of liquor should be completely avoided.

After the service I asked the minister, whose name was F. Harold Essert, if he was aware of the difference in his approach to that of his predecessor. "Yes," he said. "Men coming out of the seminaries today know more about the sciences, including the science of human relations."

He hesitated a moment. Then he grinned. "Besides," he said, "the old way wasn't working any more."

As with the sin-or-symptom category, this "desecularization" of religious morality may seem logical, inevitable, and unsurprising. The third form of the changing attitudes toward sin, however, is one that most Americans who have not been to church in some time, or who have paid poor attention, or who have been going to a church not yet affected by the psychiatric impact, will find surprising indeed.

This third development can be illustrated by an incident that occurred several years ago in a Midwestern city. A remorseful young minister confessed to a superior that he had been having sexual relations with his fiancée. The superior, in a fit of rage, damned his young colleague, whereupon the young man went out, had relations twice more with his fiancée, and then attempted suicide.

A third minister who told me this story then talked with the younger man. The young man's explanation was not unusual: he was unable to marry the girl, whom he deeply loved, because he had no money. But the situation in which the minister was placed *was* unusual. He knew that sexual relations by the announced standards of his church were a sin when carried on out of wedlock. The minister knew, too, from having been highly trained in depth psychology, that guilt can kill—as it almost had before he got there. He stared thoughtfully at the young man for a long time, and finally he made up his mind. Slowly he intoned, "When Isaac took Rebekah into the tent they were wed."

The minister had deliberately chosen a story from the Bible by which the young man might eventually rehabilitate himself in a religious sense. The story, from the Book of Genesis, relates how Abraham sent his servant out of the land of the Canaanites to find a wife for his son, Isaac. The servant traveled to the land of Nahor, and there set his vigil at a fountain where the daughters of the men of the city came to fill their pitchers. Concerned that he should choose the very maiden God had chosen for Isaac, the servant beseeched his Lord to give him a sign. He would ask one of the maidens for a drink, and if she were the chosen one, she was to respond "Drink, and I will give thy camels drink also."

Exactly this happened when the servant asked for water from a sweet and comely virgin named Rebekah. Joyfully, the servant took her to Isaac, after having first obtained the permission of her family. "And the servant told Isaac all the things he had done," the story concludes, "and Isaac brought her into his mother Sarah's tent, and took Rebekah, and she became his wife; and he loved her."

As the minister chose to interpret and utilize the story, God had obviously paid attention to the union, for how else did the holy sign pass before Abraham's servant? There is nothing to indicate that God was displeased because Isaac and Rebekah joined without benefit of a religious ceremony which, because it was not specifically mentioned, the minister assumed had not occurred.

From a religious basis, therefore, the young minister found the means ultimately to master his guilt. Because other considerations made continence desirable, he actually was able to refrain from further intercourse until he could marry.

The advising minister reflected later: "There was a time in my life when I said, 'If you don't do such and such, you'll go to hell.' I don't do that any more."

But there is more to the story than a changing view of judgment. The story involves as well a willingness to accept a specific form of conduct, heretofore considered a sin, as not a sin at all. While something of the same thing is happening in attitudes toward other aspects of sexual activity, it is with the example of premarital intercourse that we find the most eloquent illustration of the theory so frequently expressed by many Protestant ministers—that psychiatry has illuminated their own faiths to them as never before.

While it should be made clear that Catholics and even

many Protestants would emphatically disagree, certain Protestant authorities, among them Professor Paul Tillich of Harvard, Professor Otto Piper of Princeton Theological Seminary, and William Graham Cole of Williams College, contend that biblically a marriage is constituted by just two things—mutual love plus physical union. Once a man and a woman have vowed to remain together and have actually joined together, they are married in God's sight, no matter what their status might be in the church or in society. If they have vowed to wed, formally or otherwise, for as long as they live, their "premarital" intercourse is really not that at all, this view holds. Besides being the deepest expression of their mutual love, it is the very act that makes them one in the eyes of God.

Discounting for the moment the practical factors that have caused society to assume its posture regarding premarital relations, what is the biblical justification for this viewpoint? We have seen how one minister chose to find some in the Old Testament as revealed in the story of Isaac and Rebekah. As to the New Testament, Mr. Cole makes the following points in his definitive study:

In [Jesus'] ethic, that which is normative in sexual relations is *not*—as it is for society, Christian and otherwise—the external, marital status of the persons involved. Rather, the norm must be sought in inner attitudes and motives. The question must be raised concerning what sex means to the man and woman participating therein. If they are ... each treating the other as a mere body, a thing to be used and exploited as a means of self-gratification, their marital status assumes a decidedly secondary importance from Jesus' point of view.[3]

Indeed, such a use of sex for one's own selfish gratification is "immoral" in Jesus' terms, Mr. Cole concludes, "even if the

[3] *Op. cit.*, p. 27.

persons involved are thoroughly and respectably married
before the law."

Is premarital intercourse, then, acceptable? Jesus, says
Mr. Cole, never specifically answered the question. But Mr.
Cole holds with the many authorities who argue that Jesus'
emphasis on motivation answers the question itself.

What makes a marriage is the consent of the partners, their
serious intention to live together in some sense, however dimly
perceived, as "one flesh," a union of their two separate exist-
ences into still a third existence, the marriage itself. . . . The question of external status is entirely and altogether secondary.[4]

Mr. Cole points out further, in a well-documented
passage, that two of the great figures of Christian development, St. Augustine and St. Thomas Aquinas, also agreed
that the consent of the lovers to share each other's lives, plus
sexual union, constituted a valid marriage. Neither parental
approval nor church ceremony was required in their view.

Is this viewpoint extreme? Actually, it is more conservative
than that of some Protestant ministers, admittedly few in
number, who, when pressed, will go so far as to state that
intercourse is a wise and prudent step for young couples
who intend to marry.

Few who feel this way will admit it publicly, but one
who does not mind expressing his conviction in this regard
is the Reverend Frederick C. Kuether, director of the clinical
training program for ministers at the American Foundation
of Religion and Psychiatry in New York City, which was
founded by Dr. Smiley Blanton, a psychiatrist, and Dr. Norman Vincent Peale. Dr. Peale is a figure of some controversy
among the clergy, but his public popularity automatically
enhances the importance of the work done by the people

[4] *Op. cit.*, p. 29.

connected with the American Foundation. Add to that the knowledge that each year Mr. Kuether is in a position of decisive influence for young ministers; thus his thoughts are not to be taken as isolated phenomena.

It is Mr. Kuether's contention that the rites and rituals of marriage must be reinterpreted by churches in the light of psychiatric findings. He notes:

"The old church says of marriage: 'This is a relationship that does not exist until the Church says it exists. We must first lay hands upon you before you are blessed.'

"The new church says: 'The love of two people for one another is a relationship that exists. This the Church now recognizes and blesses. If this has been a relationship that has been carried on at all levels prior to the ceremony of marriage it has a better chance of succeeding than a marriage that has not been fully explored.

"We don't *urge* couples to fully explore. But when they come in for premarital counseling and in the course of the interview we ask, 'Well, what sort of sexual experience have you had together?' and they say they've had relations, we don't say, 'Bad,' we say, 'Good.'

"There is no demand that you do this. But the chances of surviving are enhanced if you do. If you don't, you have to take the consequences—which may be that you're sexually incompatible."

It is at this point that other ministers, Mr. Cole among them, would not agree with Mr. Kuether. They would contend that the problems implicit in a relationship not formalized by a wedding ceremony are greater than the good Mr. Kuether assumes would come from premarital intercourse. A complete sexual relationship between two people is a powerful experience that deeply affects the participants, this group reasons, and the relationship should therefore be

accompanied by a situation that permits the participants
to share all aspects of their life together. Furthermore, a
clandestine relationship can cause great strain and irritation
and in the event of pregnancy public disapproval as well as
grave personal problems. As Mr. Cole notes:

> Christianity... has the altogether legitimate function of
> molding the conscience after the fashion of the law of love....
> Each case must be judged on its own merits, but Christianity
> and psychoanalysis can quite properly point out that there is
> a difference between infantile love, which demands immediate
> gratification regardless of the consequences, and mature love,
> which is able to forswear immediate satisfaction for the sake of
> greater goods. Any unmarried couple engaging in sexual inter-
> course runs the risk of conception, of exposure, and social cen-
> sure.... The creation of one flesh in the biblical sense involves
> the joining of two total existences, economically, spiritually, and
> psychologically, and not just the union of two bodies. To attempt
> the one without the other is dangerous to the entire relation-
> ship...[5]

Yet it is safe to say that even those ministers who disagree
with Mr. Kuether on the *advisability* of premarital intercourse would be with him completely in refusing to condemn
a couple who engage in the act prior to the wedding ceremony. Many would also join him in this indictment: "As
long as the Church subscribes to absolute standards it just
isn't facing up to what people are like. The difference between ideal and real standards has contributed tremendously
to mental ill-health."

This grave concern on the part of certain clergymen for
the guilt and anxiety they feel they have created in people is,
it should be said once again, the force that is causing certain

[5] *Op. cit.,* pp. 304-305.

Protestant groups to quest for a modern morality encompassing man's aspiration as well as his capacities.

As we shall see next, this same concern is also causing an intense search for "healthy" definitions of man's relationship to God and to eternity.

6.

A THEOLOGY OF PSYCHOLOGY

IN Columbus, Ohio, several years ago, a young boy battered a sixty-five-year-old woman he had never seen before. When the news was broadcast a minister with a reputation for strictness approached the Reverend Roy A. Burkhart, senior minister of the First Community Church. "That ought to prove to you that Adam sinned," he said.

Mr. Burkhart's response was brief. "All that proves," he said, "is that someone withheld love from that boy."

Investigation revealed that the boy had been raised by a grandmother and two maiden aunts who were very hostile to him. In beating the sixty-five-year-old woman, he was acting out on a total stranger his aggressions for his relatives. Alluding to his colleague's obvious reference to original sin, Mr. Burkhart reflected:

"To blame some historical event for this boy's mistake is not only unfair but a malicious trick that can be played all too often on the mind of the spiritual leader. Where the more fundamental theology emphasizes original sin, what you sow you reap, ultimate condemnation and eternal lostness of the soul, the enlightened theology recognizes that the theory of original sin is a lazy excuse for not doing what love ought to do from the moment a baby is conceived."

To today's "psychological" churches the comparison is crucial. It takes bravely into account the fact that, as some clergymen have expressed it, religious definitions of man's state in creation are a menace to his emotional health. Case histories galore attest to the toll exacted by emphasis on sin, wickedness, and damnation. New understanding of man demonstrates that before he can live a full and free life he must have a strong sense of his own worth. He cannot be undermined by a negative faith.

The need for a positive religious response to the emerging dimension of man has set numbers of ministers to an active search for a more satisfying interpretation of theology for modern definitions of free will, original sin, the hereafter and even of the deity. With impressive consistency, the search has ended in the thinking of two German theologians. In one, a Protestant, the seekers find an acceptable expression of man. In the other, a Jew, they find an acceptable concept of God. In both they find the authentic religious voices of the psychiatric age.

Paul Johannes Tillich was thinking about infinity at the age of eight. Sixty years later he had become one of the most extravagantly praised thinkers of religious history. *Time* magazine, which knows how to trot out the superlatives, once projected Dr. Tillich against "the vast, sloping barrier" dividing twentieth-century Protestantism. On the plain, said *Time,* were "disciples of the liberal theology, men suspicious of absolutes and friendly to change." On the mountain were their theological archenemies, the orthodox and neo-orthodox. "They turn their faces firmly upward and preach the word in their private language; for them the world is hopelessly evil." Few men, said *Time,* ever dared commute between the mountain and the plain, but Paul Tillich did more than dare. He drew mountain and plain together.

In this accomplishment, say some, he did for Protestants what St. Thomas Aquinas did for the Catholics. Others say he "furnished a dwelling place for multitudes of homeless minds," and that his philosophy will one day reform the modern church and reintegrate modern culture. Since religious history is dotted with examples of men who, like St. Francis of Assisi, stirred their times but not, ultimately, their churches, the future of the Tillich theology should be considered in the perspective of the past. But of Dr. Tillich today some things are perfectly certain. There are few religionists in the modern camp who do not read him, revere him, and, among Protestants, at least, live by him.

If his philosophy has such transforming potential as to evoke the comments above, then to live by him today is seemingly to believe in ideas that many people would deem heretical. Yet he gives no impression of crusading militancy. On the contrary, he exhibits to a marked degree that soft, saintly quality that distinguishes the profoundly religious man—the ability to resonate with strangers. At seventy-one he is tired, harried, and, because of his reputation, set upon. Yet he achieves a deep and genuine concern not only for the issues put before him but for the questing individual who raises them; he seems oblivious to himself, as though the person were the most important he has ever known, and his problem the most significant ever posed.

A Lutheran minister's son, Dr. Tillich, as a young man, served as a chaplain in the German Army, and then went into teaching. In 1933 he was dismissed from the University in Frankfort on the Main, where he was a professor of philosophy, because of his views against the rising Nazi regime. Emigrating to the United States, he taught at Union Seminary in New York City until a few years ago, when Harvard appointed him a professor of the university, a position giving minimum teaching requirements and maximum time for research to advanced scholars. Dr. Tillich lectures at Harvard Divinity School and gives an undergraduate course in religion and culture; otherwise he is free to continue the extensive writing that, despite the depth and difficulty of its content, has excited so many people.

The explanation for this enthusiasm can be found perhaps in these few Tillich statements: "I do not think it is possible today to elaborate a Christian doctrine of man, and especially a Christian doctrine of the Christian man, without using the immense material brought forth by depth psychology. . . . Protestant theology can, without losing its Christian foundations, incorporate strictly scientific methods, a critical philosophy, a realistic understanding of men and society, and powerful ethical principles and motives. . . . Without losing the image of Christ as Saviour, the Christian must adjust the externals of his faith, his philosophy, and culture to the circumstances of the time."

Here, in other words, is a call to a theological offensive. To many churchmen accused for years, with or without justice, of reaction, the call has proved irresistible. The offensive is already under way. Says Dr. Tillich:

"We have relearned the ambiguity of human goodness, which was completely forgotten twenty years ago. Good is now a question not only of the act. We ask *why* we did what we did. What were the motives? We ask also whether we then violate the good act with other actions."

Through psychiatry he says we have quickly and efficiently "illuminated the things that religion has done to throw men into despair. Religion now sees that having to live and die alone create enough anxiety for man, and the problem should not be compounded with neurotic problems induced by condemnatory religion . . . a most terrible thing! Ministers' attitudes with respect to sex have been unendurable. There are neither biblical nor religious grounds for their attitudes. . . . The Church is learning not to make moral demands which nobody can fulfill. You cannot simply say that things are forbidden. There is love."

Here, in effect, is where a theological reconstruction begins for the clergyman who finds that his own version of theology has been both impractical and inaccurate. For to Dr. Tillich it is the individual and his unique capacities that are the holy and sacred aspects of the universe. Church-made laws are not. The power of love in human situations supersedes many of the strictures on human conduct set by certain churches. If, to take a prior example, it is a couple's inclination to have intercourse before their wedding ceremony, then there is nothing to inhibit them. If it is their inclination to abstain on the grounds that the risk of pregnancy or of discovery make continence wise, they are free to do that, too. Says Dr. Tillich:

"The essence of Protestantism need not be fixed in sacraments, ecclesiastical authority, or the churches themselves. Their outward forms must constantly change."

What does not change is what Dr. Tillich calls the "Protestant principle: the protesting voice of the prophet outside the temple, calling the people back to God and away from the formalism and sophistries of the priest."

Today the "Protestant principle" is the pre-eminent cry of the psychiatrically oriented element of the Protestant faith. To a majority of ears it is alien, but to fewer and fewer each year. To the extent that it is heard, it seems fair to say that psychiatry has made a significant impression on United States Protestantism. For the Tillich philosophy goes hand in hand with psychiatry, and to the "oriented" clergyman, one without the other is unthinkable. The reason is plain enough: Dr. Tillich's concern, like psychiatry's, is for the individual, *whose only possible sin is alienation from his true being because of hostilities, anxieties, and guilt.*

It is this concern that underlies the Tillich theology and thereby dissolves for confused churchmen the apparent contradictions between insight and faith.

Certain religions, for example, have said that we all inherit guilt at birth. Psychiatry, however, has proved that some feelings of guilt can make a disease of life. How, it has been repeatedly asked, can these findings be reconciled to the concept of original sin?

"This was always a questionable term," says Dr. Tillich. "It really meant that we all find ourselves estranged from our true being." We are, in other words, like eight-cylinder engines operating on only four; we fail to live up to our promise. When through lack of self-awareness or appreciation of our own worth, or through devotion to false standards established by society, we fail to achieve our real potential, then we are sinners. We are wasting a creature of God, ourselves.

Supposing we assume that man can move in one of two planes, one horizontal, the other vertical, Dr. Tillich wrote in a 1958 *Saturday Evening Post* article.[1] The man who moves horizontally is conforming to the demands of our competitive society, which seek to convince him that his individual worth is measured by the number of possessions he can assemble. Thus he keeps moving horizontally after more and more—a bigger house, another car—and he wonders why he is unhappy, why he remains anxious, why he feels unfulfilled. The reason is that he has ignored the vertical quest for *himself.* He has never found out who he is.

To Dr. Tillich this waste of a creature of God is the only sin, and therefore the "original" one. By eliminating all other possibilities, it rules out the question of whether we are born wicked.

[1] "The Lost Dimension in Religion," June 14, 1958.

In the matter of free will, certain religious thinking suggests that man always knows right from wrong. Psychiatry, on the other hand, has shown that the unconscious mind makes action frequently contradict ethics. What of this dilemma?

"The Christian doctrine of the bondage of the will advanced by Luther has been recognized by every step of psychoanalytic theory. We have compulsions. We have neurotic stages. We are *not* free."

There is a "tragic implication" in the birth of every child, says Dr. Tillich, because each one born must face "the negative elements of life—hostility, anxiety, and guilt." Yet we are no longer prisoner to these negative elements. Psychiatry has shown us the way to regain freedom of the will. It has taught us to recognize our bondage to these elements. Says Dr. Tillich:

"In recognizing our bondage, we see our freedom. For only he who is free can have bondage."

A third contradiction appears to exist in the promise certain religious groups extend of either reward or damnation. Psychiatry has proved that threats create a hell on earth in the form of emotional problems and mental disorders. What, the churchman might ask, has psychiatry done to the concept of hell?

"That's a symbol for a desire to do away with oneself," Dr. Tillich responds. "To say otherwise is an offense against God himself. If a minister says that there can in the context of reality be found a place which is hell then this is damned superstition. But if by hell he means a state of *life* where we are estranged from ourselves then, yes, this is hell.

"The hereafter is a word that should be confronted with the here-before. If there is a hereafter, there must also have been a here-before. But where was I before my birth? I was nowhere.

"The view of California funeral parlors that one awakens a second after death is a caricature and a blasphemy. People who think like this don't take God seriously. They are walking on the meadows. The hereafter must be demolished because it is a temporal idea and a bad symbol.

"When we are reconciled with our own true being, then we have heaven. Eternal life is *now*."

If he will believe Paul Tillich, the American Protestant of today can, therefore, seek his heaven on earth and his worth from a church that declares him an invaluable creature of God whose only sin is to make meager use of his one crack at life.

But if he is to believe in God, what, exactly, is he to believe? For such an answer, the psychiatrically minded Protestant has turned, paradoxically, to an Israeli scholar.

Martin Buber is one of those little men whose strength of face considerably enlarges him. The structure is opulently full. The brown eyes are deep, steady, and intense. A magnificent white beard makes him seem, as his interpreter Maurice Friedman notes, "like a living embodiment of an Old Testament prophet." When this visage is cast against his reputation, the effect on a first-time observer can be formidable.

Returning from such a first encounter, a Washington, D.C., Sunday-school director once exclaimed to a friend, "I've just had dinner with Moses." On another occasion a visitor at Union Theological Seminary, where Buber has lectured, blurted involuntarily, "He looks more like God than any man alive!"

Blasphemous it might have been, but the last expression came pretty close to suggesting the reverence those familiar with the man and his thought confer on Buber. His history is replete with instances of the strange things he can do to men.

A few years ago the late Hayim Greenberg, the ambassador of Israel to the United Nations, was astonished to see Charles Malik, the U.N. representative of Lebanon, and thus a foe of Israel, approaching him.

"Have you," asked Malik, "read Martin Buber's *I and Thou?*"

"Indeed I have," said Greenberg.

"Then will you discuss it with me?" Malik asked.

Thereupon, Dr. Friedman recounts in *Faith Today,* the two men, officially enemies, sat down together in the U.N. cafeteria to speak for one hour of a book that has shaken thinking men as much, perhaps, as any other in our time. Discussing it, J. H. Oldham, the foremost spokesman for Protestant unification, once contended: "I question whether any book has been published in the present century the message of which, if it were understood, would have such far-reaching consequences for the life of our time."

Buber has been compared as peacemaker to Gandhi and Schweitzer, as thinker to Maimonides. There are Protestant clergymen who contend that in the last three generations, and even more emphatically in the last fifteen years, Buber has had more influence on Christian theology than any Jew since Paul. Contemporary thinkers who have admitted to his influence include Karl Barth, Father M. C. D'Arcy, Reinhold and Richard Niebuhr, and Paul Tillich, a list that reads like a batting order starring Musial, Mantle, Williams, and Mays. By any measurable standard, Buber is one of the most important men alive. Yet it is a safe assumption that the man who would goggle at that batting order would draw a blank on the philosopher.

Who is he, and what has he done?

Martin Buber, as this is written, is eighty years old and

a citizen of Israel. He writes, lectures, and teaches through-out the Western world. Despite his years, he appears to be spry and indefatigable. In New York several years ago he was scheduled to speak at a Sabbath-night service of a Jewish congregation. That afternoon, the city was buried in snow, yet Buber, who was not well that day, insisted on walking the two miles to the synagogue. The gesture was not in his own behalf; he does not observe the injunction against riding on the Sabbath. But he had been brought to this country under the auspices of the Jewish Theological Semi-nary, which does. Out of respect to the Seminary he was determined to travel afoot.

Here, as in almost every story that can be told of Buber, is the moral that has excited such a variety of thinkers. He has evolved a philosophy of man's obligation to his fellow man, of his imperative need to be totally, not partially, aware of the other man, and to understand and accept him in terms of himself alone, not in terms of one's use for him. Man needs other men and other men him if all are to be happy and sane.

This concept of interrelatedness has become the central religious idea of the psychiatric age.

Buber evolved the idea through study, but the study itself was prompted by his own burning need. As a young man he had been a mystic who would habitually spend hours in religious exaltation. Following such a period, he was ap-proached one day by a troubled young man. Later Buber was to learn that the young man had attached an importance of life and death to the interview. During the interview, how-ever, he was not really and fully present in spirit; he answered the questions the young man asked, but he did not see be-hind the questions to the young man's true quest—which was for assurance that life was not futile, that, instead, it had meaning. Later, when Buber learned of the importance of this conversation to the young man, and of his death in World War I, he underwent a "conversion" and gave up his quest for religious ecstasy. "Since then," he recalls, "I know no fullness but each mortal hour's fullness of claim and responsibility."

Buber's concern with "hallowing the everyday" finds its deepest root in Hasidism, a popular mystical movement that had created great fervor among Eastern European Jews in the eighteenth and nineteenth centuries. Once as a young man Buber had gone through a period of spiritual and intellectual confusion. Searching widely, he had come upon a work by the Baal-Shem, Hasidism's founder.

"He recognized in himself the Hasidic soul," recounts Interpreter Friedman, and gave up political and journalistic activity in which he had been engaged in order to study Hasidic texts for five years.

"Buber's discovery of Hasidism was epochal for Western Jewry and for Western culture in general," Dr. Friedman, a dazzling scholar in his own right, asserts. "By his single-handed labors he transformed Hasidism from a little-known movement, despised and neglected by the whole of Western culture, into one of the recognized great mystical movements of the world."

It is the underpinnings of this philosophy that have provided many Protestant and Jewish theologians and even some Catholics with an explanation of man's relation to God, to his fellow man, and to himself in an age when he has partially discovered who he is. It is a philosophy that emphatically addresses itself to the here and now, rather than the hereafter. It emphasizes community and everyday life; stresses a need to love the world, "For man cannot love God in truth without loving the world." In contrast to theologies that urge continence, Hasidism urges joyousness in living, for it is despair, in this mystical view, that distracts man from the love of God and makes him a sinner. One must not be so vain as to compare himself with others, asserts Hasidism, but at the same time one must realize that in his person is a unique value which must be realized before the world is complete. Dr. Friedman cites the story of the Hasidic master who wrote that everyone must have two pockets. "In his right pocket he must keep the words 'For my sake was the world created,' and in his left, 'I am dust and ashes.' "

Buber stresses that while one begins with the task of discovering himself, his pre-eminent concern is not his own salvation, but to find a way to "let God into the world." One does things not for a future reward but to make the here and now a better place. In hallowing the everyday, one is "letting God in." The story is recalled of the Hasidic teacher, Dov Baer of Mezritch, who at one point as a young father did not have enough money to feed his child. During prayers one day the child became too weak to cry, at which point Dov Baer sighed aloud. Suddenly he heard a voice proclaim to him, "You have lost your share in the coming world." His reply was in the very tradition of Hasidism. "Well, then, the reward has been done away with. Now I can serve in earnest."

It is by serving one's fellow man that one finds his own true being *and* God, says Buber—and it is at this point that the implications for Christian as well as Jewish theology become profound.

Buber contends that we do not become real persons by being concerned with ourselves, as we like to think today. We achieve our own reality only by entering into relations with others, for it is only through the reaction of others that our own existence is confirmed. It is a form of ethical ping-pong: we cannot really be unless our being is affirmed by others, and they will not affirm us in a manner that makes us sure of our own existence unless we affirm them in a manner that totally acknowledges them for themselves. If we use them for ourselves, they are "its," just as a typewriter or an automobile is an "it," designed to serve its owner. But if we accept them for themselves, glorying in their uniqueness, not trying to mold them in our own image, then we are treating them with a respect and concern that are expressed by the familiar address of "thou."

True relationhips between individuals are the "I—Thou" relationships. If we allow the individual to be different, and still accept and confirm him, then we shall have helped him realize himself as he could not without us.

Such acceptance does not mean that one does not wish to influence another and help him change. It does mean that he says after Buber: "I accept you as you are; I confirm you as the unique person that you are before desiring to influence you."

It is not difficult to understand why Buber has caused so much ferment within the framework of a Western religion pre-eminently excited by the psychiatric dramatization of ancient religious ideas of love, acceptance, and forgiveness. As has been seen, psychiatry and religion agree, one on fact, the other on faith, that initially we must accept others for what they are, because both medically and spiritually acceptance is the beginning of redemption. Buber maintains that acceptance of the other solely for himself is not only the duty that religion and the necessity that psychiatry insist it is, *it is also the only way in which man comes to experience God.*

God, to Buber, is the "eternal Thou." He exists in the fellowship of men. Interprets Dr. Friedman:

> God wants to come into the world through our loving relation with the people we live with and meet, the animals that help us with our farm work, the soil we till, the materials we shape, the tools we use. "Meet the world with the fullness of your being and you shall meet Him," writes Buber. "If you wish to believe, love."

Christianity, John Knox Jessup has pointed out, is founded on "a tremendous historical fact . . . the Incarnation of God in Jesus Christ, eternity's great intervention in time." Beyond the belief in God's presence through Christ, however, lay Christians and many theologians have assumed salvation and redemption to be in a world beyond their own, in which they would at last meet God. For a Christian to accept Buber, therefore, is profoundly to suggest that Christian theology needs to be brought more into the here and now. This is the basis for the excited contention that Buber's influence on Christian thought, particularly on Protestant thought, has been epochal.

"He brought God to earth, or man to heaven," insists one interpreter. "He destroyed the gulf between heaven and earth."

Buber was lecturing at a synagogue one evening a number of years ago when a member of the congregation demanded to know why the philosopher had so greatly influenced the Protestants. Buber's simple response said much. "Ask the Protestants."

Dr. Friedman insists that Buber has never tried to extend his philosophy to others. They have demonstrably reached for him. Church leaders who believe that too much emphasis has been given to spirituality see in Buber a chance to relate religion to life as it has not been related in recent times. J. H. Oldham, for example, says, "I am convinced that it is by opening its mind, and conforming its practice, to the truth which Buber has perceived and so powerfully set forth that the Church can recover a fresh understanding of its own faith and regain a real connection with the actual life of our time." [2]

To be sure, not all Christian theologians have reached as

[2] Joseph Houldsworth Oldham, *Real Life Is Meeting* (London: The Sheldon Press; New York: The Macmillan Co., 1947), pp. 13-16.

far. Many from the more literal faiths would blanch at the
thought that the existence of God can be known mainly
through the interactions of men. But they *would* accept the
idea that seeing another person through his eyes, experienc-
ing his side of the relationship, jumping into his skin, as it
were, is a function related completely to acceptance, and
is therefore not only a psychiatric ideal but a religious pursuit
of the highest order.

Such an ethical function is a cause for dreams and wishes.
One dizzies at the prospect of its mightiness applied to our
contemporary social and political situations. Buber himself
is proof that the application can be made. His attitude toward
Jesus, for example, is a superb illustration of the crucial
ability to see the other side.

"Buber has recognized and pointed to the tremendous religious significance of Jesus as possibly no Jew has heretofore
done while remaining firmly planted on the soil of Judaism,"
Dr. Friedman contends. To prove his assertion, he quotes
two observations of Buber.

"From my youth onward I have found in Jesus my great
brother. That Christianity has regarded and does regard Him
as a God and Saviour has always appeared to me a fact of the
highest importance which, for his sake and my own, I must endeavor to understand. . . . My own fraternally open relationship
to Him has grown ever stronger and clearer, and today I see Him
more strongly and clearly than ever before. I am more than
ever certain that a great place belongs to Him in Israel's history
of faith and that this place cannot be described by any of the
usual categories." [3]

On another occasion Buber said:

I firmly believe that the Jewish community, in the course of

[3] *Two Types of Faith,* translated by Norman P. Goldhawk (London: Rout-
ledge & Kegan Paul, 1951; New York: Macmillan Co., 1952), p. 12 f.

its renaissance, will recognize Jesus, and not merely as a great figure in its religious history, but also in the organic context of a Messianic development extending over millennia, whose final goal is the redemption of Israel and of the world. But I believe equally firmly that we will never recognize Jesus as the Messiah Come, for this would contradict the deepest meaning of our Messianic passion. . . . There are no knots in the mighty cable of our Messianic belief, which, fastened to a rock on Sinai, stretches to a still invisible peg anchored in the foundations of the world. In our view, redemption occurs forever, and none has yet occurred. Standing, bound and shackled, in the pillory of mankind, we demonstrate with the bloody body of our people the unredeemedness of the world. For us there is no cause of Jesus; only the cause of God exists for us.[4]

As Dr. Friedman notes in his comprehensive study, *Martin Buber: The Life of Dialogue,* "The Christian sees the Jew as the incomprehensibly obdurate man who declines to see what has happened, and the Jew sees the Christian as the incomprehensibly daring man who affirms redemption in an unredeemed world."

Yet by his actions no less than by his thoughts Buber dissolves the contradictions, and emerges as one of the two most creative and useful thinkers to a religion that is attempting to reconcile itself to Freud. To speak of accepting sinners is to recall the figure of Buber, spiritual leader of German Jewry in its hopeless battle with nazism, accepting the Peace Prize of the German book trade less than ten years after the liquidation ended. To an audience of Germans in Frankfurt he recalled that several thousand Germans had killed millions of his people "in a systematically prepared and executed procedure, the organized cruelty of which cannot be compared with any earlier historical event." How could

---

[4] Quoted in Ernst Simon, "Martin Buber: His Way between Thought and Deed," *Jewish Frontier,* XV (February, 1948), p. 26.

he who could not and would not forget this atrocity stand before those in whose name it had been committed, and accept their prize?

Because, said Buber, the greatest duty of man has always been to fashion one humanity out of the hostility of separate groups, no matter how impossible seemed the task.

"I must obey this duty even there, indeed just there where the never-to-be-effaced memory of what has happened stands in opposition to it."

With historical allowances, could not these have been the words of Christ?

7.

THE HUG OF THE BEAR?

O F THE 350,000 clergymen in the United States today, approximately 235,000 have pulpits, according to the *Yearbook of American Churches,* meaning that they also have parishioners whom they serve in the historic pastoral tradition as counselors in time of need. Protestant ministers contacted in a recent survey by Samuel Blizzard of Princeton Theological Seminary, under a grant from the Russell Sage Foundation, reported that they counseled on the average of three hours a day. There is basis to assume, therefore, that individual clergymen are counseling 750 hours and the clerical fraternity as a whole *175,000,000 hours* a year.

Since this is a projection with many unscientific assumptions, and since there are no extensive studies to authenticate these incredible figures, it is best to account for all sorts of possibilities for error by reducing the figures by nine tenths. This still leaves us with an imposing 17.5 million hours in which ministers, priests, and rabbis give counsel. Assuming that these hours are accounted for by individuals who return several times, we arrive finally at a most cautious estimate that in 1959 somewhere between 3,000,000 and 4,000,000 disturbed Americans will be seeking help for marital, parental, emotional, economic, and even psychotic problems from their churches and synagogues.

Many explanations have been suggested for this contemporary phenomenon. One is that it is not a phenomenon at all, but merely an age-old custom that because of our growing awareness of psychological conflict is simply receiving wider attention and publicity today. Unquestionably there is something to this explanation; better reporting techniques have the superficial effect of giving an epidemic proportion to all sorts of social developments. The reporting on cancer is a good example of this; while it may be that the increase in the incidence of the disease is due to an increase in smoking and in the pollution of air by industry, it is just as true that more doctors are able to recognize cancer symptoms today, and that there are more agencies interested in collecting the data.

Certainly there is nothing new in the pastoral counseling function, per se. As Paul B. Maves noted in *The Church and Mental Health:*

It is popularly assumed that the Church is concerned only with things of the spirit while the physician is concerned with things only of the body and the psychiatrist only with things of the mind or perhaps of the emotions. Too often it is assumed that the interest of the Church in spiritual healing or in ministering to the sick with a view to restoring health is something new that has come into the Church. Mental health is thought to be the concern of the secular priest, and not of the religious ministry.

We need to remember our roots in order to gain perspective upon our present practices ... while there is something that is new in the modern movement for pastoral care in the churches, actually what is happening is a rediscovery of the whole gospel for the whole man and a recalling of the Church back to an inherent concern which has existed from its foundation.[1]

[1] *Op. cit.,* p. 41.

But other factors are unquestionably at work to add impetus to the modern pastoral counseling movement. It has been suggested that the pace and uncertainty of our times are giving more problems to more people, and thus creating a greater need for help than ever before. Another factor to be considered is the population swell and its shift to the suburbs where a need to integrate has been at least part of the reason for the heralded religious revival.

A final factor, and a subtle one, is the reluctance of many people to take their problems to a psychiatrist or psychologist. Despite the wide recognition of psychiatry's endeavors in the last fifty years, there exists today not only a great deal of suspicion toward the psychiatrist, but a persistent feeling that a stigma attaches to psychiatric care. Pastoral counselors frequently report their visitors as saying, "I couldn't stand to have my friends see me come out of a psychiatrist's office." Another common observation by people explaining their presence in the religious counselor's office is, "I didn't think any psychiatrists were Christians." As the American Foundation of Religion and Psychiatry, the mental hygiene clinic created by Dr. Norman Vincent Peale and Psychiatrist Smiley Blanton, noted:

"The religious auspices of the Religio-Psychiatric Clinic have encouraged visits from many persons who, because of fear or prejudice, might not otherwise have sought or received psychiatric treatment."

There is considerable latitude in the feeling expressed for the pastoral counseling movement. It has been hailed on occasion as "a most amazing move toward the reduction of mental illness." It has also been viewed in terms somewhat less kind. One wary observer describes the burst of church enthusiasm for counseling as "the hug of the bear," crushing what it embraces. Whatever the judgment, the pastoral counseling movement is one of the dominant factors in United

States religious life today, and churches are working hard to provide facilities and trained clergy to meet people's needs.

There are six different versions of pastoral counseling available to the individual with a problem, according to George C. Anderson of the Academy of Religion and Mental Health. These are:

The average clergyman, trained or untrained in the insights of depth psychology, who counsels whenever someone comes to him with a problem.

The clergyman trained to some degree, who has organized his pastoral counseling duties to a point where he sees people during specified hours every day, or on certain days each week.

The clergyman who has become a specialist and who is employed by his church to be, exclusively, "the pastoral counselor."

The church that has actually set up a clinic and has engaged the services of clinical psychologists and psychiatrists to work with the church's staff of ministers. About forty such clinics exist in major United States cities today. Their prototype is the Religio-Psychiatric Clinic established in 1937 by Dr. Peale and Dr. Blanton. A nondenominational mental hygiene and pastoral counseling clinic, the American Foundation, as it is known today, employs fourteen psychiatrists, two psychiatric social workers, three clinical psychologists, and four counseling psychologists. Eight ministers and four "pastoral interns" (also ministers) complete the Foundation staff. Clinic services are free, but voluntary contributions are accepted "from those financially able as a means of extending this service to others." Services include "diagnosis, counseling in moral problems and human relations; psychiatric testing; and psychotherapy to maladjusted and disturbed individuals."

Religion plays an important role in the work of the clinic [the Foundation notes in a report], since all ministers and therapists recognize the healing power of religious faith, and the need by most individuals to arrive at certain fundamental beliefs and goals which give meaning and value to life.

Religious counseling is used most frequently to remove unconscious, morbid feelings of guilt. It is valuable where problems are seemingly rooted in religious conflict.

If the therapy is to be extensive, the clinic usually refers patients to other sources. This is apparent by its record of visits, in which in one year alone the clinic saw 1,567 persons a total of 5,295 times, or an average of fewer than four visits per person.

A fifth type of pastoral counseling service is that which has been established by the local Protestant Council of Churches for members of a community. The council employs trained pastoral counselors who work either alone or with psychologists or with psychologists and psychiatrists both. There are perhaps a dozen of this variety in the United States. In this category might also be placed the counseling service offered by the Boston University School of Theology. Also a community effort, the service employs ten pastoral counselors, all of them ordained ministers, all of whom have specialized in psychology and pastoral counseling through postgraduate study, clinical training under supervision, and actual pastoral work.

A final form of the church-sponsored counseling outlet is the guidance clinic established by a church, which then takes no part in any of the counseling or therapy. An example of this type, of which there are only a few in the country, is the Westwood Community Church clinic in Los Angeles. Forty psychiatrists staff the clinic on a voluntary basis.

Lest any impression be given that pastoral counseling is exclusively a Protestant function, it should be recalled that the project to create courses in mental health for use in divinity schools, sponsored by the National Institute of Mental Health, is being undertaken by Yeshiva University in New York City, and Loyola University, a Catholic college in Chicago, as well as by the Protestant Harvard Divinity School. Indeed, enthusiasm for pastoral counseling is so high among Jews that recently Dr. Henry E. Kagan, chairman of the Committee on Psychiatry and Religion of the Central Conference of American Rabbis, called for a form of "confessional" for Jews.

Dr. Kagan noted that "serious-minded Jews" frequently complain that "we do not have something in Judaism similar to the confessional booth in Roman Catholicism." This complaint, he noted, proves that confession is a need that is "natural to every human being."

By confession, he said, he did not mean a ritual that "may become mere dogmatic routine where neither the conscious nor the unconscious motive for a sinful act can be explored in the few minutes a penitent talks to a concealed confessor."

"To fulfill the expressed need of the congregant to be heard," Dr. Kagan said in a speech reported in the New York Times, "modern Judaism should more vigorously encourage the training of rabbis in the ancient and classic religious art of pastoral counseling, which is now being revived, especially in Protestant circles, because of the impact of modern psychology on theology.

"Wherever rabbis are matured by training for such counseling, synagogue members should be advised that their rabbis are available for personal confession."

Irrespective of the actual amount of counseling being done, there is considerable concern among observers in all three faiths that the counseling clergymen first be trained in depth insights. Counseling in and of itself need have no relation to psychology or to a real understanding of people, and it is the contention of Mr. Anderson of the Academy of Religion and Mental Health that in far too many cases it doesn't. He estimates that while 50 per cent of the ministers and rabbis are attempting to use depth insights in their ministries, as few as 10,000—less than 15 per cent—have been adequately trained to use them well.

Mr. Anderson notes, however, that opportunities for training are increasing each year, and he predicts that within ten years at least 40 per cent of all clergymen will be incorporating insights into their ministries.

What are these insights, and where are they obtained? While many so-called pastoral counseling courses offer students a few weeks of observation at playgrounds, or a week in various courts of justice, the real training is generally carried on in a clinical setting. Theological students and ministers usually study in hospitals or mental institutions under the supervision of psychiatrists, psychologists, or trained pastoral counselors.

As to the insights themselves, a few principles and examples will show how a trained clergyman can learn to understand behavior and even symptoms in terms not only of their outward form but of their inner meaning. He would, for example, be made aware of a psychiatric principle as enunciated in *The Church and Mental Health* by Dr. Gotthard Booth of New York City:

In health, each personality tends to express itself particularly through one psychological or physical function. If this function ceases to be satisfied in relationship to the environment, the organism becomes sick and is forced to express the personality symbolically. In some diseases the connections are obvious. For example, unbending attitudes are connected with arthritis, needs for individualized human contact with hallucinations, and mother dependency with alcoholism. In other illnesses the connections become understandable only through more specialized study of the physical and psychological functioning of the organism. Susceptibility to infection and the effectiveness of immunity reactions often can be related convincingly to frustrating life situations.[2]

The pastoral counseling trainee would learn, further, that some deep and unresolved unhappiness can lead to aggressive action directed against society. The Reverend Carl R. Plack, a leading pastoral counseling authority in the Lutheran Church, recalls a minister who once had to deal with a bank robber with a harelip. Assuming that the criminal had a gripe against the world because of his deformity, the minister arranged for him to have the harelip removed by plastic surgery. The assumption was right: the bank robber reformed.

"A man acts aggressively because he has been maimed by somebody or something," declares Canon Charles W. Stinnette, Dr. Loomis's associate in the Department of Religion and Psychiatry at Union Seminary. "A pastor must be willing to accept a person who has such aggressions and at the same time not be maneuvered by them." He cannot, in other words, permit himself to become inflamed by the individual's unsocial conduct.

"Suppose you've been counseling with a man, trying to get him to talk, and after two or three hours the man says, 'Why don't you say something, goddammit! You're just like my father.'

"Get angry at his profanity and you'll lose him. You've got to keep your temper and say, 'Tell me more. Come on, out with it.'"

A story of this nature brings to focus an exceedingly important question—that of the dangers involved when a clergyman counsels a troubled individual. Under ideal circumstances, the minister spends a few hours with the individual,

[2] *Op. cit.,* p. 9.

by which time he will either have helped him, or will have recognized, as did Canon Stinnette in the case above, symptoms of a deep psychological conflict, and will have arranged for him to be treated by a psychiatrist.

"The pastor might spend three or four hours to see if this man can deal with his conscious problems," says Mr. Stinnette. "I would strongly recommend that the pastor not take it beyond four, five, or six hours. You get into problems of transference, dependence, and distortion of the relationship of the rector."

What Mr. Stinnette is talking about is the chemistry that occurs between two people genuinely concerned with a solution to the problem of one of them. The psychiatric method, it will be remembered, has as its basis the acceptance and understanding of the individual, regardless of what he has done. Whether the recipient of his troubles be a minister or psychiatrist, the troubled individual develops a regard for the person who is helping him. He comes to depend on him. In some cases, he even comes to love him. These states of being must, of course, be resolved before the individual can achieve a permanent cure. But they are states of being that an untrained man cannot successfully resolve, and one reason is that he himself becomes deeply involved. "In counseling, you almost get the feeling of being a junior God," Psychiatrist Emanuel Honig of Beverly Hills, California, the former rabbi, declares. "The minister becomes involved personally, subjectively."

Despite these warnings, however, clergymen in some instances have become so enthusiastic with pastoral care that they have actually begun to do therapy. According to Mr. Anderson, the Academy of Religion and Mental Health regularly receives complaints from county medical boards to the effect that ministers are attempting to deal with psychotic disorders.

"Clergymen who endeavor to deal with emotional prob-

lems without sufficient training or knowledge of emotional
disorders may, with the best intentions, be as guilty of malpractice as if they were dealing with a cardiac or respiratory
illness," Mr. Anderson states.

"It is essential that clergymen understand their limitations.
Psychiatric knowledge informs counselors when they can help
and when to refer an individual for more specialized assistance."

Another danger is that the clergyman will not really recognize what's wrong with the individual. Instead, he will
accept a surface manifestation as the real illness, and pray
with the individual for relief. On its surface, the statement
of one minister active in the pastoral counseling movement
seems to make sense from the religious viewpoint. "I counsel
with people for just one purpose—to find out what to pray
for," he declares. Yet according to one psychiatrist who has
been working with clergymen for more than twenty years, and
whose position does not permit use of his name, this very
act of prayer can sometimes reinforce the individual's sense
of guilt.

"The error of some clergymen is not so much a matter of
excess as it is of malpractice," he declares. "The fault arises
when the minister fails to bring the individual's problems
into a remediable situation. He thinks he knows what's
wrong with the individual. When he prays with him for
deliverance from this supposed disturbance, it's an acknowl-
edgment that the disturbance is genuine."

The psychiatrist cited the case of a woman whose son had
been killed in an accident while she was away from home.
For six years after the accident she had been inconsolable,
plagued by an abiding grief and sense of guilt. In despair,
she had sought the "mysterium of her church." When prayer
failed to assuage her guilt, she had turned against all religion.
The mistake her clergyman had made was in taking her

grief at its face value, for in analysis her psychiatrist uncovered a completely unsuspected condition, one of inadequate relationships with men generally. Separated from her husband and unable to find another mate, she had unconsciously come to expect in her son the fulfillment of all her dreams for happiness with the opposite sex. Her son's death created the necessity of dealing with her problem realistically, and it was for this reason that she was aggrieved.

While some clergymen do abuse the counseling function, their actions by no means deter more and more psychiatrists from seeking an effective alliance with religion. There is a growing awareness among doctors that religion, rather than being an "obsessive neurosis," can be a tremendous ally in the fight against mental illness. By suggesting some cosmic view, it offers people a certain measure of relief from "ontological" anxiety, the normal fear of living and dying. The church can teach people to accept themselves as creatures of worth, and to live in the context of a world of other people with whom they must relate to achieve their own "true being." Ideally, therefore, the church can be of help in both therapeutic and nontherapeutic situations. Practically, however, the church's record has, in the opinion of some critics, not been ideal.

One such critic is Dr. Iago Galdston, chairman of the Committee on Information of the New York Academy of Medicine, and a well-known psychiatrist who has been identified with the reconciliation of religion and psychiatry for a quarter century. Dr. Galdston tells of treating a number of patients who were without an "effective superego." In lay terms this means they had no ideal image of themselves, and therefore no standards by which to live. Says Dr. Galdston: "They had developed into an order of maturity that did not embrace any concern with . . . the meaning of life and its achievement in a deep relatedness with others, either with one's intimates, or with mankind at large.

"They sponsored ideas and movements. . . . They related themselves to 'the arts,' and to schools of thought, but not to people. . . ."

As therapy, Dr. Galdston determined to make use of religious resources. "In conspiring with the patient to help him acquire a superego, I attempted to steer him toward the 'communion of fellowship' promised by the church," he relates.

What happened? His patients, Dr. Galdston recalls, "were proffered the communion of fellowship, but only at the price of dumb conformity. The church demanded complete submissiveness and the unquestioning acceptance of its word. This not as an ultimate but rather as the initial condition. To put it bluntly, it soon became apparent that the minister was more interested in defending his doxies, his faith, and his beliefs than he was in helping the man in search of his soul to find it."

This very criticism, as we shall see next, has already caused a minor reformation in one important church.

8.

GOD, FREUD, AND SUSAN PETERS

SUSAN PETERS *was a Hollywood actress who rose to fame and showed great promise from 1943 to 1945. She was married in 1943. On New Year's Day in 1945 she was seriously injured in a hunting accident which resulted in total paralysis from the waist down. Although the doctor told her she would never act again, she determined that she would return to the stage; within two years she was acting in the movies and on the legitimate stage, all of her roles being those which could be played from a wheel chair.*

In 1946 she and her husband adopted a baby boy only a few weeks old. In 1948 she divorced her husband, because, she said, she wished to give him his freedom. It was during those years that she toured the country successfully in The Barretts of Wimpole Street.

In 1949 and 1950 she conducted a television program. In 1951 she became less active, and her death occurred in 1952. The death was headline news throughout the country because her doctor said that although she had died of a kidney disease, she really died because she had lost any desire to live longer. It was her lack of interest in living which slowly and naturally caused her to succumb to an organic disease. Although some friends showed a tendency to dispute this state-

ment, the doctors were convinced that a desire to live would have enabled her to live.

Upon this terse summary is based a strange, challenging and disruptive adventure for members of the Protestant Episcopal Church of the U. S. A. Lasting but two days, it is designed—and has succeeded in its design thousands of times in the last few years—to knock pious people from their religious moorings.

The story of group life centered in church fellowship is as old as the country. Its return in recent years as a meaningful, significant aspect of the pattern of religious revival in the United States is quite new. More than dances, cake sales, and bingo parties, group life activities today are conceived with a purpose. In some groups, the purpose is guidance, as with that of the First Community Church of Columbus, Ohio, whose "Guidance of the Whole Person Program" had been instrumental, to 1956, in getting 650 of its young men through the armed services without a single discharge for psychoneurotic reasons, and in compiling a record of more than three thousand marriages with only seventeen divorces.

In other cases, where trained counselors are available, the purpose of the group is therapy. In these sessions several members of the church, whose only qualification is that they have an emotional problem, meet together to seek a cure. Under the direction of a leader, frequently the clergyman himself, hostilities are adroitly brought to the surface, then explored.

The Parish Life Conference is neither practical nor, technically, therapeutic. It is a religious experience en masse. But it is in many ways the most exciting group activity within American churches and synagogues today.

It was in 1946 that leaders of the Episcopal Church decided that the educational program of their church was "dead."

They were critical not only of what the Church was teaching in relating faith to life, but of the assertive, uncompromising manner in which it was being taught.

An effort was then begun to revise all activities relating to child and adult education. Mute at first, it is today the dominant note of the Episcopal Church, and makes this group one of the outstanding examples of psychiatrically induced change in the last twenty years. Leaders of what even the lay members now call "the revolution" frankly attribute their awakening and motivation to new scientific insights, and particularly to the insights of psychiatry and depth psychology. Underlying the activity is a recovery by ministers of the need to listen instead of preach, forgive rather than condemn. The Reverend David R. Hunter, director of the church's Department of Christian Education, and one of the truly significant figures of the "revolution," says: "This imperative to listen has had far-reaching effects on the clergy, and we got it directly from psychiatry."

In the story of Susan Peters the Episcopalians have, they feel, found a device that illustrates in an unforgettable way what the love of one's fellow man must be like before it can be considered religious. Such love, they readily admit, is identical to that employed so dramatically by psychiatrists in therapeutic situations—the acceptance of individuals for what they are, loving them in spite of the fact that they might be unlovable.

"That's just what Christ meant," an enthusiastic minister insists, "and we'd forgotten all about it until we were reminded by psychiatry."

The story of Susan Peters is told at a critical point during a weekend retreat attended by anwhere from ten to forty lay members of the Episcopal Church. A rector who is unknown to any of the people attending—there are usually no more than five from any one parish—and who is skilled in group dynamic techniques uses the story to illuminate the difference between what is and what ought to be in terms of the parishioner's relation to his fellow man. The goal is to make each parishioner see that he has been paying lip service to love, that love as he metes it out is usually on his own terms, and that if he himself is ever threatened—if it becomes hard for him to love—he usually stops loving.

Before the conference is over, the individual has discovered in a personal and shattering way that periods of threat to himself are precisely the times when he must love others if he is to consider himself a truly religious man. The manner in which he comes to this revelation is unforgettable.

They came for the weekend to the Episcopal Center at West Cornwall, Connecticut—an attorney and his wife from Danbury, two young businessmen and their wives from Bridgeport, two young grade-school teachers from small Connecticut towns, a doctor's wife from Essex, and a caretaker's wife from the state university.

They were, without exception, devout. Only one of them, the wife of one of the Bridgeport businessmen, had not been an Episcopalian all her life, and she had converted from Catholicism at her marriage. Not one of them had an idea of what the Parish Life Conference was about, and only one, the husband of the converted Catholic, had any real desire to be there. He was, he later admitted, anxious to show a group of Episcopalians what a good Episcopalian he was. All the others had dutifully come because their rectors had urged them to go.

Later, every one of them was to admit that he had prepared some pious statements he felt the conference leader would want to hear. But the leader—and the conference conception itself—was way ahead of the participants. For it is an assump-

tion of the conference that on Friday evening every participant will walk devoutly into a trap.

"I'll start out being permissive as all get out," the leader,
the Reverend Joseph Johnson of West Hartford, had told his
observer, the Reverend Sherman Andrews of East Hartford,
earlier. To that end he was wearing a checkerboard plaid
shirt to which was pinned a name tag bearing the simple
legend, "Joe Johnson." Actually, his natural mood was one
of outgoing enthusiasm. He rarely endorsed with a simple
"yes" if he could say "You can bet on that."

After dinner the group gathered on sofas and chairs in
the spacious living room which, with its Steinway piano,
shelves of books, fireplace, and warm lights, gave very much
the feeling of being "at home."

Joe said: "We're going to ask a few questions about ourselves and our relation to the parish this weekend. You're
going to work hard, but there won't be any pressure. By
Sunday at noon we'll be finished; I hope you'll be wiser, but
I know you'll be more tired."

Then Joe wrote the first question on the top sheet of a
large pad of paper mounted on an easel: *What is the basic
purpose of my parish church?*

"Why don't we break up into two groups? Is that okay
with everyone?" It was.

While the two groups were framing their response, Joe
confided to his observer, Sherman, "They're going to brag
tonight. They'll say a lot of wonderful things like 'fulfill
our spiritual needs' or 'teach our children'—that sort of stuff.
They'll go to bed tonight feeling this conference is a breeze,
they've got all the answers. Brother!"

When the reports had been made, Joe, who had led a
number of PLC's, proved he knew what he was talking about.
For the first group said that the aim of the parish church
was to "fulfill the individual spiritual needs of the parish-

ioners," which included "worship, Christian education, and service," and the second group reported the aim as "devotion and education."

Joe dutifully wrote the responses on a large pad of paper. For a moment he mused. Then he said, "The sex life of the fruit fly in the fourth generation is interesting, but I wonder if it means anything to us. What do all these words mean?"

Morton, the Danbury attorney, a heavy-set man both outspoken and assured, broke in: "The basic purpose of the parish church is to see that the individual educate himself, find out why he's a Christian, what he should do, and spread out the Lord's message for others. You've got to instill these things in people so they radiate out to others, and make the church significant, broaden its position in the world. I don't know about the rest of you, but that's what devotion is to me—doing something to make the church strong. Worship is something else."

His confident speech made Ellen, the caretaker's wife from the state university, radiate. A woman past sixty, she wore her hair in a bun, and her face was plain except for powder. She had the manner of a person who was used to church gatherings of any sort and thrived on them. "Oh, thank you, thank you," she said. "You've cleared something up for me already. I had been thinking of devotion and worship as the same thing. Thank you."

Encouraged, Morton went on. "It's easy to go to church Sunday after Sunday, but it may not mean a thing. It's much more than going to church every Sunday. You've got to work for the church, because the church can do its work only through individuals. That's the only way it can stretch out its tentacles and broaden its work."

The Bridgeport businessman who had been eager to attend spoke up. He was a smooth individual who on first encounter barely avoided seeming unctuous. "Any church that hasn't taught us why we go to church has failed of its purpose. That purpose is to enable you to make Him know you are glad to be in His house."

"But you've got to know *why* you're doing these things," Morton said.

"I disagree," said the Bridgeport man, whose name was Olin. "Man doesn't have to know a thing. Worship is by instinct."

"When I worship God I feel my own inadequacy," Morton said.

"Well, don't we all?" came the chorus. "That's why we're here."

Ellen, the white-haired lady, whose sole resource, it seemed increasingly, was her own experience, said, "It has to come to each individual at a separate time. I remember when I was a young married woman, I cut my finger once and my whole hand got infected. Because of one finger I couldn't use my hand at all. I realized then that the church is just like that. Every single member has responsibilities. We go along, we feel good, but we don't know why we do it, especially sometimes when working for God comes hard. But that's when you're really giving devotion to God."

There then began a momentous period of silence. It went on and on, and as it did everyone seemed to grow more and more uncomfortable. Finally Bob, the other Bridgeport businessman, broke the stillness with his first contribution of the evening.

"I'm surprised that Joe doesn't have anything to answer."

Joe, the minister, smiled at Bob, but he remained silent. This did not help Bob, who was to portray himself in the next few days as an individual who had been content to accept without question the hand-me-downs of his religious environment.

Ellen talked to herself a moment. Then she said aloud, "I still say we're supposed to spread the Gospel, and live by the Word. Teaching, preaching, and healing. Christ put so much value on the individual, the lost sheep. We go to church to gain strength to go out and spread the Word of God. . . ."

"What Word of God?" Molly asked, a little sourly. A schoolteacher, she was young and fresh and pretty, and of all those present she appeared to have the most inquisitive nature, the most independent outlook, and easily the largest capacity for seeming irreverence. She was already annoyed by the glibness of the others.

Ellen straightened. "Are you trying to trip me up on words?"

"I just want to know what the words are," Molly said.

"All right. We have to start off by learning to love God. You don't love something you don't know anything about . . . I'm doing all the talking . . . well, I'm sorry, but I just get excited about these things. . . . We're trying to love God, that's all. That's what our parents taught us. That's what we learned in the Bible."

As Ellen's voice trailed off, everyone looked at Joe. Slouched in a deep-upholstered chair, Joe looked back at them and smiled.

"No matter where we go, we seem to wind up with people," he said. Then he rose and wrote the second question on the large paper pad: *What is the basic need of man?*

"Same as the fruit fly?" Olin wisecracked, and those who heard him laughed. Bob laughed very hard. Then he said, "Boy, we better get some psychologists in on this one."

They split again into two groups and as they drifted out of earshot, Joe said to Sherman, the observer, "We're getting lots of watermelons here. Now we'll start to thump 'em and see if they've got anything. Boy, that Olin sure carries a load of hostility. Someone's gonna beat him up on that before we're through."

They came back into the living room twenty minutes later and Ellen, having apparently warded off the intimation that at least one person in the room considered her a windbag, said, "Whew, this is wonderful." On the other hand, Morton, the effusive Danbury attorney, had become pensive. He seemed to sense that things were not going well.

Joe said confidently, "I'm sure that when we've heard the two reports we'll know what is the basic need of man."

The first report held that man's need was "a good spiritual relationship with other people under the fatherhood of God." The second report said much the same thing: "We must love God and must feel that God loves us." There was no opposition to the theory that man's need was—in some form—the love of God.

"I have a three-year-old girl who doesn't love God," Joe said.

"What?" Alice, Bob's wife, said. She was a somewhat strident and domineering woman. Now there was a ring of challenge in her voice that exactly expressed the quizzical grimness of the others.

"I said I have a three-year-old who doesn't love God and doesn't know that God loves her."

"Sure she does," Alice said.

"She does?"

"Sure. I got a little girl, too. She loves God."

"How do you know?" Joe said.

"Because I tell her all this stuff."

"Oh," said Joe. "Why do we need the love of God?"

"Because we need to have good relations with other men," Olin interjected smoothly, "and we are united with them through the love of God. One man on earth is meaningless."

"I need God," Morton said, "because I need somebody who will listen to me, somebody I can get into seclusion with."

"We're expressing our love of God through loving our fellow man," Olin said.

"That's it! Brotherhood!" Ellen shouted. "Oh, I'm talking too much. I feel the basic need of man is what the Law says. Love God and our neighbor. We must do that before this world will ever be as God wanted it to be. There'd be no quarrels. We'd all get along. . . . Please, I get so excited. . . ."

The silence now lasted a full minute. Morton, Olin, and Ellen all seemed to expect their answers to achieve recognition from Joe. But the minister said nothing.

"Oh, please, Mr. Joe, say something," Ellen shouted finally.

But again no one in the group, not even Joe, said anything.

"Oh, Mr. Joe, don't just sit there. I wish I could see the inside of your head."

In the third silence that followed, Morton exhaled cigarette smoke with great vigor and noise.

At last Joe spoke. "My daughter doesn't know the love of God. She doesn't know that God loves her," he repeated.

"Oh, of course she does," Ellen said. "You're just saying that. A fine man like you." By now she really believed that Joe needed her assurance.

"Let me change the context a little," Joe said. "I make $25.00 a week. I'm an alcoholic. I spend all my money on liquor. I don't give my daughter any food. I beat her up. . . ."

"Nine times out of ten this child won't know the love of God," Alice said. "But if she meets just one good person she can love God."

"Can she?" Joe said. He smiled. "Well, we've been talking in a very generalized way for the last few hours. We've said a lot of nice things. They've been very *safe* things. When you go to bed tonight, I'd like to ask you to think in the silence of your own room, 'How far would I go personally in meeting the needs of an individual in a specific situation? How much would I let it cost me?' "

The trap had been set.

"Susan, we've got a job for you," Bob, the Bridgeport businessman, announced.

By means of role play, Bob was making a pitch to "Susan Peters," the crippled, heroic, reputedly embittered actress, to join his group in fellowship. "Susan" was really Bonnie, the Essex doctor's wife, whom Joe Johnson had coached a little earlier that morning. He had asked Bonnie to portray Susan as aloof and unresponsive, even though inwardly she was apparently a miserable and lonely person who needed to be reached by others. The theory held further that because no one had reached her, Susan had died. Illness had been a factor, but doctors insisted she had lost the will to live. Her illness might otherwise have been cured, they said.

Joe had said nothing about this interpretation of Susan's inner problems to the conference members. To them he had said instead: "Is it possible that we might be able to give Susan Peters life? Let's see if there isn't some pitch we can make for giving this woman the will to live. Remember this: It's role play, but it's real. This is life and death we're dealing with."

Now "Susan," played to the hilt by Bonnie, was seated with her legs on an ottoman, smoking a cigarette and coolly regarding the young man and his committee who had come calling. "You have a job? What sort of a job?"

"You won't have to be in front of people, Susan. We're a group from the PTA and we've got a lot of children with speech impediments who don't get the proper training. We thought with your background you'd be able to help them. So we want you to head up the teaching."

"I'm sure there are many speech-impediment teachers,"
"Susan" said.

"But we thought with your wonderful background, we're
sure we'd see results," Bob said.

"Well, I'll give you a check, but I really can't make an
effort. You see what I am here." "Susan" indicated her use-
less legs.

Then Martha, a schoolteacher and a close friend of Bob's
wife Alice, rushed to Bob's support. "But these children
need professional help," she said earnestly. "They can't really
go out in the world. There's a four-year-old who can't say
his name. By the time he's seven he'll be in a mental institution. They need training. They need you."

"I have many burdens. I just can't do it."

"We can cut it now," Joe broke in. "You haven't saved
Susan Peters."

The second group tried a series of individual approaches.
Ellen posed as a former schoolmate. "Do you remember
Charley, the blessed boy? He was leading us down a hill on
a bobsled and when we came to a tree he put out his feet
so the others of us wouldn't be hurt and broke both his legs.
The dear boy . . .

"Well, Susan, we feel you belong here. We need you so
much. We know you've reached a point where you need us.
We need you. We may annoy you sometimes, but try to
remember the nice things about us and come to sit in church
and smile and give us a little inspiration, won't you? Well,
good-by, it's been wonderful seeing you again, and you're
looking just wonderful, you really are!"

Molly came in with an offhand spirit. "Hi. You got a cup
of coffee? I'm dead."

"James," said "Susan" to an imaginary butler, "coffee for
the lady."

"Listen, Susan, I'm having a party next week and I'm

stuck on a salad dressing. You have a reputation as a good cook. Can you help me out?"

"I'm sure Janet in the kitchen can do something for you."

"Listen, Susan, what I really wanted to talk to you about is, a couple of us have coffee once a week and we'd like very much for you to join us."

"That might be nice, but it's really such a relief to just sit here and not have to go anywhere."

Then came Olin, posing as "Father Carmody."

"Susan, we're glad to have you back among us. The old ties always bring people back, don't they?"

"It's quiet in the country," "Susan" said.

"Thank you," he said, ignoring her slur. "Susan, we have problems here, one hundred and twenty-five families full of problems. I hope some of your insights will help us solve them. You remember Alice Smith? Well, a few weeks ago her husband lost his job and he took to drinking and he's become an alcoholic. They have two kids, and I was wondering if you would be willing to send her a little word of condolence. Just that much would mean something to her."

"I'm sure her friends would be much more in a position to help."

"The friends are doing all they can."

"I really have no interest in the situation."

"Okay," said Joe, breaking in. "Susan died again."

The outburst of hostility which followed was so volcanic that for a while individual remarks could not be distinguished. Of the ten participants, only one, Molly, remained silent.

"If she's that miserable, let her die," Alice said, her voice finally rising above the din. She laughed at her wisecrack.

"Maybe you're right," Olin said. He, too, found her remark humorous.

"You almost felt as though there was no hope," Bob said.

"We thought we might at least have planted a seed," someone said, and everyone agreed.

"No person ignores appeals like that," Alice said.

"We didn't want to be precipitous," Morton said. "We wanted her to feel that she belonged. We'd give to her and later she could give to us."

"She closed her mind to anybody, and to any appeal. She was bitter. She didn't let God do a thing for her," Ellen said. There was real bitterness in her own voice.

Joe stood up and wrote a single word on the paper: *Judgment*.

"I ignore appeals all the time," Molly said, breaking her silence. Suddenly she seemed very much alone, set off from and confronted by an angered mob. The animosity toward "Susan" perceptibly shifted to her.

"You can't ignore a specific appeal," Alice said.

"Let's face it, it didn't come off," Joe said. "Why?"

They looked at what he had written on the paper.

"If we can't have an opinion without judging, how can we do anything?" Ellen said. "There you are. I don't know."

"It's pretty hard to figure out in fifteen minutes what to do," Olin protested. "It's a long-term proposition."

"How long would she tolerate it?" Joe asked.

"I don't see how she can come to the conclusion that she shouldn't help a bunch of children with speech impediments," Bob said petulantly. He was very righteous.

"Listen, we have to be careful in our approach with a woman like that. Lots of people would hate her," Ellen said.

"Are you sure it was Susan Peters who was being judged?" Joe said.

Then Molly spoke up firmly. "Let's face it, as a Christian church we failed to meet her spiritual needs completely."

This time no one fought her.

"Where are we?" Ellen said pitifully.

There was a prolonged silence. The sense of distress was acute.

"Well, I'm going to judge and I'm sorry," Ellen said finally. "Susan's need was to be a little less selfish in her thoughts."

"You know," Joe said, "I'm reminded of *The King and I* where the King says, 'Etcetera, etcetera, and so forth.' "

The silence now was absolute. It was broken when Morton noisily exhaled his cigarette smoke.

"She was selfish. She wanted to be a martyr," Olin said.

"What was Susan's need?" Joe asked reflectively.

"I have no idea how to approach her, but she needed love," Alice said.

"She had to realize that she wasn't the only one with a problem," Martha said.

"You know the saying about how you can push someone to the water, but you can't make him swim," Joe said.

"Maybe we should have pushed her wheel chair into the water," Martha said angrily.

"We need a professional psychologist to go into this thing," Bob said.

"We thought for a while a drama group . . ." Ellen said.

"She'd have to be awfully gracious," Molly said.

"She obviously was not," Olin said.

"I don't believe Joe has the solution," Bob said. "Otherwise he would have told us by now."

"There obviously was none," Olin said. "She died."

Molly spoke up again. "You know, I don't think we really cared about her as a person, but just as a soul who needed to be saved. We all talked to her in our frame of reference. We said if she doesn't wear the size sweater we want her to, she's no good.

"How many of us would have gone in the first place?" Molly asked.

"How many Susan Peters are there in your own church right now?" Joe asked.

"Listen, in our church if you weren't born into it all they do is nod at you," Alice said.

"In our church they don't even nod at you," her husband Bob said.

"Her basic need has already been mentioned and nobody picked it up," Joe said.

"Who said it?" everyone asked.

"That's for me to know and so forth," Joe said.

"Was she a psychology—a psycho case or something?" Bob asked.

"She was just like you only a little more beat up," Joe said.

"I still say the love of God is offered to anyone who will take it," Ellen said.

"That sweater shrinks," Joe said.

"Should we have told her we appreciate what she's done in making a comeback after her accident?" someone asked.

"That would have fallen flat as a wet noodle," Bob said.

There was a silence.

"Let's stop here," said Joe.

At the afternoon session Molly began to sound like the Devil's Disciple. Actually, she had become a little fed up with her fellow Episcopalians. She had also come closer than anyone to figuring what the game was all about.

When someone suggested that Susan Peters had to be led to Christ, Molly rejoined, "Who's Christ? You can't take *Him* too seriously. After all, He said we should be perfect and we all know we can't be that."

When someone else suggested that it was their duty to save Susan Peters, Molly said, "Why bother? After all, death is a good thing to have happen if your problems get too big."

"We've got to learn to be better salesmen," Ellen said. "Perhaps we didn't send the right people."

"We sent everybody here," Molly said. "She wanted *My Fair Lady* and we gave her the PTA."

Martha, more sensitive than her friend Alice, was also beginning to understand her failure. "Perhaps it was because this was the first time we ever tried to help anyone," she said in a soft voice.

"What do we want to help Susan Peters for? We need a disagreeable cripple in our church?" Molly said.

Alice turned on Molly, completely missing Molly's facetiousness. "I don't go along with your ideas at all. I wouldn't be a Christian if I felt the way you do. If you're a Christian, you help people with problems."

"We're the problem," Martha said softly.

"What?" Alice said.

"I said we're the problem. We're not going to admit it, because *we're Episcopalians,* we're so much better than anyone else. But that wasn't Susan. That was us."

Before it had been simple frustration with a problem that could not be solved. Now, throughout the group, there was a look of embarrassed revelation, like that of people who have played their joke on an old man and then come to a realization of their meanness.

Molly spoke:

"I don't know if this story is out of place or not, but I remember when I was going to college, I decided I'd be very holy and go to Communion once a week. Boy, I felt wonderful. My first two classes in the morning I just tingled all over. And then one day I realized that the day I took Communion was the one day of the week I had a cup of black coffee on an empty stomach."

"But we need Him," Ellen murmured. She had taken out a handkerchief and was holding it to her face.

"You're telling a fib," Molly said.

"The church needs every single soul," Ellen insisted.

"To do what?" Molly said.

Joe intervened. "We've been talking about what ought to be," he said. "Let's contrast it with what is."

"Have we gotten nowhere?" Ellen asked.

"If we could only be perfect," Molly said. "Go to a local bar and not have a drink . . ."

"I know a Methodist minister who went into all the bars in New Haven and never had a drink," Ellen interjected. "He was asking all the boys at Yale why they drank."

". . . not exceed the speed limit. Be kind to widows and orphans."

"It's very important to be kind to widows and orphans," Ellen said. She was near tears.

"What we need is humility. We've got to get off our perch, admit our frailties," Olin said.

"And Susan died," Joe said.

"Can't the minister help us?" Ellen asked.

"Don't put the pig on the minister's back," Joe said.

"We should ask divine guidance," Bob said.

"We do that every day," someone said.

Morton shifted heavily in his chair. Although initially he had been the most aggressively outspoken participant, it had been some time since he had last spoken. Now he did. "Nobody's more confused than I am, but at the risk of being unpopular, may I suggest that we've been using a lot of clichés? Bring God to our house. Bring God to Susan. That's silly stuff. Something else is needed. We didn't try very hard to put ourselves in her position. We've got to find a premise."

"We've got to get her to God," Bob insisted.

"That doesn't mean a thing to me," Morton said. "Maybe we can put her in an airplane and get her a little closer, but that's not going to help her. Her problem isn't doing something for others, it's doing something for herself."

Joe sang, "If I had the wings of an angel." Then, looking at Morton, he said, "The man says I'm sick and tired of words, I want to grapple with something. What do you say?"

As they broke for dinner, Alice said to Martha: "I'm going to quit the church."

"I'm beginning to wonder if I had any idea of what God's all about. Anybody else feel that way?" Morton's wife Janet said at the evening session. "You go along with a pattern all your life and then something like this jolts you. I'm confused."

Dinner had been a wild, boisterous meal. Alice, acting as though shot with adrenalin, had carried on a burlesque of her vow to quit the church and had, unknown to herself, served as everyone's emotional outlet.

By the sharp nature of the inquiry, these people had all exposed to danger the religion they had brought to the conference. Regardless of how incomplete this religious belief might have been, it was something each of the individuals prized and relied upon. Psychologically, it is exceedingly risky to take away an individual's ideals without providing a replacement. Quite possibly the boisterous joviality at dinner had been an attempt to fend off this danger by denying its existence.

"We've seen that the cliché answers weren't enough," Joe said as the evening session began. "We're confused now, and a little hostile. Tonight let's ask ourselves this: 'Did we love Susan? If so, how? If not, why not?' "

For several minutes there was a sense of almost total loss. Finally Morton said, "Instead of trying to handle the problem the way we want, why not handle it the way Susan wants?"

"Without God?" Molly asked.

"That's a possibility," Morton said.

It was then that Janet asked whether anyone else was confused about God.

Alice responded: "I *feel* God. I go to a weekday service and I can feel Him. I know He's there."

"Do you have to go to church to feel God?" someone asked.

"I can feel Him in my own bedroom . . . I mean, my own home."

"Each of us is a Susan and together we need the church," Martha murmured.

"What about people who aren't baptized? Christians have no special value—" Molly began.

"—merely because someone squirted them with water," Joe finished for her. Then, switching elements with hardly a breath, he said, "A piece of charcoal taken out of the fire won't burn."

"Isn't that what we were trying to do? Bring Susan back into the flame?" Bob asked.

"The church can be the lousiest Rotary Club you ever wanted to see," Joe said. "That doesn't light any fires. I wish all the women's auxiliaries and all the men's clubs would fold up all this claptrap. It's just so much wasted emotion. Hold a dance and make $60.00. Hold a cake sale and make $20.00. Nuts."

By now Ellen was putting her well-crushed handkerchief to her face every few seconds. At Joe's statement she looked as though she would cry into it. "Oh, no. He's wrong," she murmured.

"Get away from the sideshows and get to the main tent," Morton said.

Olin and Alice, both from the same parish, turned to one another and said simultaneously, "The Couples Club."

"Suppers? Bazaars? Hell, go to the Kiwanis or Rotary,"
Joe said. He looked around the room for a response, but
there was none. The group was hiding in silence. "The bed
of coals is laid," he said; "let's get it lit."

After a long time, perhaps three minutes, Joe said, very
softly: "I don't want to be shocking, but you're dead."

He turned to a diagram he had drawn; it consisted of
three circles: the circle of God was uppermost, the circles
of the church and Susan were below and parallel to one
another.

"What's wrong with this diagram?" he said.

"There's no link between the church and God," Olin
said.

"We got God up on a pedestal," Bob said.

Suddenly Alice, Bob's wife, had had enough. "Maybe our
church has been all wrong," she cried out. "Maybe we were
taught wrong as kids. Maybe we shouldn't have been taught
we shouldn't do this and we shouldn't do that. Maybe we
shouldn't pray. When I have a problem I want to be alone
and I take it to the Lord."

"Where does Bob fit into this?" Joe said gently. For two
days now he had been keenly watching Alice dominate her
husband.

"I'm the only problem she's got," Bob muttered.

Alice almost leaped from her chair. "Hey, Joe," she
shouted, "you're going to have us divorced before we leave
here." She sank back into her chair. "I'm just telling what's
good for me, that's all. Maybe I'm just selfish that way."

The outburst had shocked everyone. Again there was one
of those momentous silences. Then Joe said, "Olin said
something important a few minutes ago, but none of you
heard him."

"I'll say it again if it will edify anyone," Olin said. "It
doesn't edify me. I said there's no link between God and

church. We set Him in His heaven and we go about our business."

Joe stood and flipped the page. There was a new drawing, with God in one circle and Susan and the church in a second circle below. Between the two circles were arrows going each way. "Is this any better?" Joe said.

"This is the way it should be," Olin said.

"*Can* be," Joe said.

"But what about Susan Peters? What do we do about her?" Alice said.

"We'll have to go home and meditate on that," Olin said.

"I hope He hears you," Joe said.

"Wait a minute," Morton said. "That diagram still isn't right. What we need is one circle with God, the church and Susan all inside."

Joe drew the diagram and then left the room to make a phone call. Instantly the group rearranged itself and began talking heatedly.

"I don't see how a man can be like that and be a minister," Bob said. "If he's the minister, let him tell me the answer."

Someone suggested that they should have prayed with Susan Peters.

Ellen said, "I think if we came in and said a prayer to Susan Peters she'd have a fit."

"Well, what *are* we going to do?" Alice shouted. "We've got to be nice to her. It's our duty."

"You're nice to me just once because you have to be and I'll spit in your face," Molly said.

"I have such a splitting headache," Ellen said.

Then Ellen began a long account of the work her church was doing, of how her rector had admonished the women to serve and many who hadn't done a thing before had begun to "bake and sew."

"And Susan died," Molly said.

Joe came back into the room. "Where were you?" he said.

"Ellen was telling us about her parish," someone said.

"Well, I was just saying . . ." Ellen began, and repeated the entire story. "There was no question that they were try- ing to serve. They—"

For the first time since the conference began, Joe appeared to lose patience. "Thank you," he said loudly, "and Susan died."

A few seconds passed. Then Olin said, "Well, Morton, you were saying the diagram—"

"What's the matter with you people in this room?" Joe said. "I just hit someone over the head and not a one of you moved to protect her."

"We didn't feel we ought to," Alice said.

"We didn't agree with her," someone said.

"But you got to protect her," Joe said.

"We don't want to be clobbered," Martha said.

Ellen, who had not yet recovered from the sudden attack, said, "I was scared."

"One of the things we can take away from the conference is the thought that we can become sensitized to the needs of people," Joe said.

"Olin tried to cover up," someone said. "He started asking Morton a question."

"But he wasn't thinking of rescue," Joe said.

"I wasn't," Olin said.

"Susan Peters," Joe mused suddenly. "On the outside suave. Inside, a tragic, brokenhearted, empty, lonely soul. What does the church have to say about the *unlovable* soul?"

With this word, Joe Johnson had released the trap that for more than twenty-four hours had held ten laymen of his own church prisoner. The following morning they were all to gather like shipwrecks who had been plucked from the sea—depleted, reverent, retrospective—and speak familiarly of

the "revolution" that was under way in the Episcopal Church.
Until that point none of them knew what this revolution was
or entertained the idea that he was, in fact, participating by
his presence at the conference. But the key that releases
the trap and sends the Episcopalians home, hopefully, to
mature and meaningful church service, is the idea that they
must "love the unlovables." Through the device of the Parish
Life Conference, Episcopal leaders are able to show that all
men, whether lovable or unlovable, have a psychological
need for a "redemptive fellowship." Depth psychology has
offered substantial new proof of this ancient religious assumption that all men are terrorized by the prospect of
separateness. Thus in one sense, at least, the Episcopal Church
is able to speak with scientific justification for its position that
the presence of God through the Holy Ghost redeems and
binds men in a saving fellowship.

"You know, Joe," a member of the group was to remark
later that evening, "it's amazing that after 1,900 years of
Christendom, the Episcopal Church has to send its members
to mountain retreats for the weekend to find out what Christ
was really saying."

"But that's the way it is. Until 1946 we were a church
that didn't understand its own treasures. We were saying,
'This is the way! This ought! That ought!' Now we're saying,
'This is the situation, and here's what we feel we have to deal
with the problem.'"

On Sunday Joe was to tell the group that the "revolution"
in the Episcopal Church had been assisted by "every good insight that came out of psychiatry and psychology."

"We've used them all, with joy," he would add.

But on Saturday night, after more than a day of insistent
battering, the group had yet to be reconstructed. This is
how it was done:

"What does the church have to say about the lonely, un-lovable soul?" Joe mused.

"We're all a little like that," someone said.

"Aren't we!" Joe said. *"And that's the only way we'd ever reach Susan Peters, by acting like we are.* But you wouldn't reveal it to her. You were too pious to admit it.

"If we're ever going to do any good, we're going to have to stop being do-good, pious clods, aren't we? God has only you to work through. If you are just you, no more, God can work through you.

"You rejected Susan Peters on very pious grounds. *You were rejecting her.* She wasn't rejecting you."

"Look," Alice said, "Martha and I are good friends. It's different with her than with a stranger. Her troubles are mine."

"If she's living with your husband?" Joe said sharply.

Alice recoiled. Then she spoke. "What you're saying is that there is the love of God in us for each other. It should be that way with a stranger?"

"That's right," Joe said. "And even with friends. Love has to be more than friendship, because if the friendship is threatened, if you are threatened, the friendship breaks down.

"No one was able to forgive Susan Peters for the threat Susan Peters presented to her. 'I'm Susan Peters. Who the hell are you?' she was saying. Does the church have anything to say about that?"

"I knew a woman in New Jersey who forgave and forgave," Ellen said. "Her husband cheated on her, and she took him back. We all said what a wonderful wife to forgive like that."

"And I say what a wonderful husband to accept forgive-ness like that!" Joe declared. "When a woman cheats on her husband and comes back and they sit down and talk it over, then I say what a wonderful wife, because she wants to find out why she did what she did and not do it again.

"I think the sin of adultery is unfortunate. How can you truly love your husband or wife if you commit adultery? That's why it's mighty grim in the eyes of God. But I think the sin of dealing with Susan Peters the way we did is much more unfortunate."

"But we know what adultery is," Alice said. "We were ignorant of Susan Peters."

"*That's the sin,*" said Joe. "We do it all the time. *We are ignorant to the needs of others.* We are unable to deal with others. We want love, but can we love others? We can't."

And at ten fifteen on Saturday night the answer was finally on the floor, when Bonnie, who had acted the part of Susan, concluded, "It means accepting each person for what they are."

"That's it," Joe said. "We're going to love to the limit of our ability and ask God to increase that ability. We're going to love the sinners in our midst."

Looking around the room, one could be certain that in terms of its working meaning this was a new thought to everyone there.

"We're going to set aside the old man of the ought, the try, the failure, and put on a new suit. We're going to accept ourselves as we are right now," Joe said.

"It seems as we abandon the guideposts, the laws, we have to replace them with something," Olin said. "With love, eh? That takes a while getting used to."

"It cuts the heart out of the angles, doesn't it?" Joe said. "But if duty is done without love, it ends in death."

"I'm amazed we made such idiots of ourselves. We just walked right into it," Molly said.

The next day Joe was to suggest adroitly that loving the

unlovables meant that Olin would have to fight in his vestry someday to make Negroes accepted in the parish. Now, in the silence, he contented himself with a single thought.

"I might say," he told his rapt listeners, "that you're playing with fire."

9.

"IT'S LIKE BEING BORN AGAIN"

DIRECTORS of Christian education of a number of Protestant faiths were in the midst of a discussion at Conference Point Camp in Williams Bay, Wisconsin, a few summers ago when one of their number, a pretty woman in her late twenties, suddenly fled from the room in tears.

These religious leaders were all skilled in psychology, so when the young woman returned they wisely said nothing, hoping that she would explore her problem with them when and if she felt like it.

They did not have long to wait. The young woman recalled that for four days the conference had been discussing ministers in a way that could almost be considered irreverent —picking apart their motives and actions, pointing out ways in which they could hinder education, giving specific instances of erroneous, dangerous abuses of theology.

Had the young woman been offended? Not at all. The cumulative effect had simply been to surface a suppressed antagonism for a minister she had known as a child who very much resembled the sort of minister the conference had been discussing. So strong and ambiguous had been her emotions that she had suddenly found herself crying.

Her ambiguity is a significant characteristic of a major

development. For whereas religious Americans tend to vener-
ate and rely upon their clergy, at times making a father image
of them, few figures in the United States have been so completely analyzed, criticized, and modernized in the last twenty
years as have our Protestant ministers.

Both in appearance and performance the "modern" minister of today is vastly different from his predecessors. His
work is different. His concept of his own role is different.
As we have seen, his thoughts about sin tend to be different.
But above all the image he presents to his parishioners is
different.

Today the once-common conception of a minister as a
powerhouse figure preaching the definitive Word as though
he had daily telephone conversations with God is definitely
passé. One authority at the National Council of the Churches
of Christ has tidily summed up what happened: "We have
reduced the status of some high-status individuals."

To a lesser extent this same situation exists within the
rabbinate. "The rabbi no longer views himself as a vast store-
house of religious truth," a Hebrew Union College professor declares. "The answers are not necessarily bound up in
this great body of revealed truth of which I am the cus-
todian."

The modern clergyman is as enlightened theologians have
always wanted him to be: a leader who by temperament and
training is equipped to share with his parishioners in the
search for a meaning to existence and the development of
human resources for the realization of that meaning. He does
not preach. He listens. He does not inject. He draws out. He
is vastly more accessible and informal. Often he is ad-
dressed by his first name. And in committee meetings or discussion groups his opinion is generally no more important
than anyone else's.

How he changed is quite a story. It could hardly be told without psychiatry, for in psychiatric findings lie its beginnings.

At the heart of the story are two seemingly obvious but only recently accepted conclusions. First, a clergyman is a human being, capable of and vulnerable to all the drives, virtues, and foibles of other human beings. Second, the religious life, for a number of reasons, is particularly attractive to human beings with unconscious problems.

Clergymen with a natural ability to understand the uniqueness of their positions and the influence they are capable of exerting over their congregations have always existed in abundance. A high percentage of ministers has always been mature, intelligent, and healthy. But religious bodies have come to realize in the last two decades that numbers of ministers have tended to use their offices as outlets for their own emotional difficulties. And where this has happened religion has suffered.

"It would be interesting," says the Reverend George Anderson of the Academy of Religion and Mental Health, "to measure the amount of hatred that emerges from the mouths of preachers Sunday after Sunday. Such hatred is often symptomatic of the preacher's unconscious guilt, hostility, or anxiety—in other words, of his emotional illness."

Many authorities, both in religion and psychiatry, now agree that young men entering the ministry in too many cases expect to fill a moralistic, puritanical role. As Dr. Loomis of Union pointed out, good seminaries always tried to disabuse students of these notions, but were largely unsuccessful until psychiatry gave them the tools and words with which to work.

The authorities would agree that ministers who ultimately distort religion usually come from homes in which normal life in childhood had been impossible. Their early problems may be reflected in their ministries—even though they are far from being full-blown neurotics.

For example, a minister may be excessively rigid in observing the customs and traditions of his church, and may seek to impress upon his parishioners that violation of these customs would lead to dire consequences. Psychiatrists would immediately suspect this man of coming from a home where he was terribly insecure and frightened. In the rigidity of church custom he finds the security he lacked as a child.

Other ministers may stress to their congregants the need to suffer. Their view, represented as the correct religious view, would be that life is a miserable experience, and that only in death would be found the reward of bliss. In such a ministry it can readily be seen how concepts of essential wickedness and original sin would tend to be emphasized. Condemnation would be held out for anyone who did not conform to the viewpoint of the minister. Here the psychiatrists would suspect that the minister is seeking to be a martyr, and is suffering from a need to be punished. He is, in other words, a "masochist."

Still other ministers may find in their positions a gratification for so simple a need as that of attention. These ministers were usually pampered as children by their parents. With the loss of the parents, the ministers in this category look for a substitute, and find it in an admiring congregation. Their needs may be gratified by the mere feeling of position. On the other hand, they may feel compelled to cut a figure for themselves to assure admiration. Consequently, they develop into authoritarian ministers laying down the law.

In all of these needs to gratify a desire carried over from childhood the ministers find a unique opportunity in an ecclesiastical life.

The tragedy is that the theology they offer tends to be colored by their own needs, and to differ in varying degrees,

depending on the strength of these needs, with ideal interpretations.

Even the great number of healthy ministers who enter the
religious life for purely spiritual reasons are subjected to a
temptation that is both unusual and strong, many churches
now concede. With ordination, the new minister inherits
power, the power to either scare or assure, to advance or
retard, to do good or bad, in short to affect the lives of the
people with whom he deals. History is replete with illustrations of personalities that have been altered by sudden power
in politics, business, and other forms of secular life. The
ordinary problem of power and its effect on personality
applies no less to the religious life—and recognition of this fact
has been responsible for a surge of activity in religious circles
in the last twenty years.

Although the fact is never broadcast, a number of ministers
have already completed or are in analysis. The trend is also
apparent in seminaries. Many students are now sent to psychiatrists for examination and therapy each year.

The reaction of those who have been through analysis
is profound. "Any man who's had analysis," says Canon
Charles Stinnette of Union, "knows what it means to be born
again." The Reverend Frederick C. Kuether of the American
Foundation of Religion and Psychiatry, drawing on his own
experience, declares: "Too many ministers try to convince
themselves they are like Jesus Christ. They think this way
because they're scared, scared of normal thoughts and feelings
they can't accept because they think it's wrong to feel that
way. This is more than fear. Fear can be proper fear—like
fearing a drunken driver. What I'm talking about is the
nameless dread that goes beyond any fear.

"For example, I was brought up in the most orthodox
manner. God was watching every movement I made. The
boom's going to lower—that's the way I felt. Now that I've

had analysis I know that the so-called 'bad' thoughts occur in all of us throughout our lives, and they're not sins to God at all."

Chaplain Otis Rice, until recently of St. Luke's Hospital in New York City, speaking out of a background of thirty years' work with troubled people and in the training of ministers for pastoral counseling roles, foresees the day when all ministers will have had analysis. "I don't see how ministers are going to get by without it. Only when he knows and thus neutralizes his own prejudices can a minister properly help those who need it."

Inevitably, the aim of the minister seeking help and of the people trying to help him is the state of detachment in which he is able to listen instead of preach, advise rather than judge, urge rather than condemn. As Maurice A. Riseling, the clergyman-psychologist, put it: "As soon as a minister is more secure himself, he doesn't need to become God to the people."

Perhaps the sharpest expression of the effect analysis has had on a particular clergyman's attitude comes from the Reverend Roy Burkhart of Columbus, Ohio, First Community Church. Mr. Burkhart, it will be remembered, was the pastor who refused to draw from the beating of an old woman by a young boy the moral that all men were wicked. Having told the story of the young boy's subsequent rehabilitation, Mr. Burkhart confessed that he had not always acted as responsively to people's needs. Asked what had changed him, he answered memorably: "All I can tell you is that I used to condemn and now I don't, and the reason I don't is because I was analyzed."

But rather than in psychiatrists' offices it is in the seminaries themselves, and in hospitals where candidates for the ministry and rabbinate go for clinical training, that the greatest drama of the changing belief is being acted out. Very frequently the drama revolves around the old problem of the nature of God. For the actors involved, it is powerful drama.

One who has observed it many times is Dr. Dana L. Farnsworth, Harvard University's director of health services, who teaches at the medical school and the divinity school as well. "If a man can become skilled in depth psychology, he is more secure than ever before," Dr. Farnsworth notes. "But in between he goes through terrific anxiety as his concept of God and his own role changes. There are men who survive as religionists, after all, only by their rigidity.

"A man challenged by the new view will try to hold on to his old values because he feels the new values threaten him. The older person feels that God is an old man with a long beard and a blue nightshirt sitting at a control box where He manipulates all our activities. The man who's had training won't know *what* God is."

Dr. Honig of Beverly Hills, the former rabbi who still teaches courses in theology, declares, "My students are amazed when I speak to them of a loving God. They sort of feel I'm pulling their leg. They say, 'We like this, but this isn't what Father taught us.' They had thought of God as vengeful, punitive. God will punish—this is what they usually heard. Most of them feared God. They hadn't thought it out; they had merely heard, and too often, from their rabbi."

It is when they move to the clinical training phase of their seminary life that the young ministers and rabbis have the kind of experience that offsets the generalizations they have made about God. They find out, to borrow the analogy of one who did, that the relationship of God to people is very much like the relationship of the therapist to his patient— complete acceptance. While, just as in psychotherapy, there will come a time when the individual will be expected to confront and fulfill legitimate demands, the initial relationship, the gift, is a state of grace in which "God comes to us even when we can't get to Him. We are accepted by God even though we may be unacceptable."

In the clinics the young ministers discover for themselves that wrath sickens and love heals. It turns them to an agonizing scrutiny of their own roles and, at times, to a bitter review of the neurotic religionists who shaped their views. Wrote one young clergyman of his home-town minister:

"His attitude was warm and friendly on the surface, but . . . hostility often came forward in his preaching. He was anti-dancing, anti-movies, anti-smoking and drinking, anti-Catholic, anti-Jewish, anti-liberal Protestants, anti-sex, and so on. One could almost say that he preached against everything except his own denomination, saving souls by faith through grace, and his own family. Most of the church members respected and feared him. My mother once told me that he adopted his children because he was too good to have children of his own. He was the symbol of the perfect Christian."

Obviously, such an individual, a caricature of a good clergyman, is not equipped to deal with the problems of other people. He has far too many of his own. In a counseling situation, furthermore, he could not be judgmental and effective, both, for a judgmental pastor who sets down the Word cannot help an emotionally troubled individual who needs, above all, to be heard.

Take the case of the belligerent young vestryman who had just gotten a good scare about his health. It is not an actual case, but rather a make-believe one that was used with considerable success several years ago at the College of Preachers of the National Cathedral in Washington, D.C., to prepare ministers for real contact with disturbed parishioners. The vestryman, "role played" by a minister, is in his thirties, has always gotten ahead by pushing people around, and considers himself quite a figure in his parish because his family is a fixture of the church. But one day, according to the script, he goes to the hospital for a routine checkup and, without being told what's wrong, is held for several days.

When he gets out, he makes a beeline for his rector (played by another student minister). He's anxious, and needs help. But because of his need to seem important he is unable to deal honestly with the rector. Instead of admitting he's anxious, he attacks the rector.

He criticizes the church: It's dirty. The choir's poor. Membership is down. It's not doing so well as it used to with the old rector.

"Before the rector knows it," says an observer, "the man has badgered the hell out of him." At times the acting gets so realistic that the participants forget the situation is make-believe, and respond accordingly.

What does the clergyman do? Does he rise up in his wrath and, invoking his vault of power, the *mysterium tremendum* that sets him apart from ordinary men, crush his antagonist? Or does he realize that the man confronting him is sick, and that his best course is to let the man push him around now, and explore the causes of his explosion with him later?

What, in other words, do ministers do, not only when their patience as human beings but when their sense of moral values is assailed by the weakness of their congregants? Do they pounce and judge, or listen and understand?

Observers of the religious scene are convinced that where the former was all too characteristic of clergymen twenty and thirty years ago, the latter becomes more and more common today. Such a process of change does not occur at once. Nor does it occur without some high drama. For while "listening" seems a simple enough technique, it sometimes involves a turning inside out of the clergyman's role.

One of the best descriptions of this process comes from the Reverend Robert Leslie, youthful, energetic associate professor of pastoral psychology at the Pacific School of Religion in Berkeley, California. Mr. Leslie's observations are invaluable for one reason above all others: he has been through the entire process. By his own admission he began his ministry as a judgmental authoritarian preacher. Then he came in contact with psychiatry, and his entire attitude changed. He saw God and his faith in a totally different light. Today he watches the identical process occur over and over again in young men he trains. This is what he has to say:

"Most of our men come to us with the idea that theirs is the didactic authoritarian role of telling people, 'It's in the Bible. Therefore it's true.' This is bad, because it doesn't work. It's a graft that doesn't take."

The root of the problem, Mr. Leslie agrees, lies in the type of religion people learn as children. They get the attitude, he says, that God is the judge, just as the parent is the judge. When these children grow up to become ministers it's Mr. Leslie's job to change their minds.

"Some of our ministers resist. But if we can get them in the clinics face to face with the patients, into the mental hospitals and jails and delinquent homes, we can ask them how their theology relates to the needs of this person—this girl who's a prostitute and mentally ill whose present circumstances are the result of a whole series of situations over which she had no control. They'll learn that they don't start out by condemning her. They start by loving her. Then when they get their own parishes and a girl comes to them and says, 'I want to get married' and they start talking and find out that she's four months' pregnant—then they'll know what to do.

"The clinical work requires a total rethinking of God. If a man has taught a loving God and then turned around and condemned people, there's a separation between his theology and his working philosophy of dealing with people.

"It's really a conversion when a man begins to look upon people with understanding rather than with condemnation. It raises a lot of very basic questions about sin. To what degree is man responsible? How far can you hold him responsible? Let's understand what forces are in his life.

"When a minister accepts these ideas, his preaching changes. He no longer stands in the pulpit and denounces. He talks about how all of us get involved in these problems. He becomes a much nicer guy to live with."

Of his own experience he says:

"For me this was a tremendous change from orthodox religion. Once I preached that if you don't do this and that, God will get after you. Now I preach that God loves you, no matter what."

Perhaps as well as any man could be, the Reverend Mr. Leslie is aware of the difficulties involved in transition. "These things don't happen overnight," he notes. "Where a minister has been judgmental and laying it on the line to where he is accepting and forgiving is a long, long way."

10.

RORSCHACH AND THE CLERGY

FATHER WILLIAM C. BIER, S.J., a professor of psychology at Fordham University in New York City, has the look of a man whom nothing would faze. Although he is not an especially big man, his face has a massive character that, coupled with an unending intensity of expression, gives one a definite opinion that he will be the central force in whatever proceedings he is involved.

But on a hot day in July 1953 thoughtful Father Bier was a worried man. He was about to make the most important speech of his life.

In his hand was a paper summarizing five years of intensive independent work based on even more years of constant research and study. Although he was completely confident of the truth of his findings, Father Bier had an idea that he was going to knock his audience for a loop.

He knew from personal experience that Catholics generally were suspicious of psychology. Moreover, this was no general audience of Catholics. Seated in the auditorium at Fordham at an Institute on Religious and Sacerdotal Vocations were nuns, brothers, and a sprinkling of priests.

In a few minutes he would declare to his audience that persons applying for admission to the religious life were seldom prompted by purely supra-natural motives. He would assert, further, that according to his findings the religious life was peculiarly attractive to young people seeking escape from emotionally turbulent pasts. Finally, he would declare that the only way to populate the demanding religious life with sound, dedicated individuals was to subject all candidates for admission to a series of psychological tests, to send those applicants about whom the tests raised questions to psychiatrists for deeper probing, and to drop anyone about whom the examinations showed any doubt at all.

Father Bier knew that he was flying in the face of two classic Catholic viewpoints. Many leading Catholics had always insisted that the choice of religion as a vocation had an element of divine mystery to it "hard to understand for anyone who has not experienced it," impossible of expression by intellectual formulas. It involved a sacred Catholic belief that "vocation is but one instance of the mystery of God's grace and man's free cooperation with grace." How, it had been repeatedly asked, can you measure something so essentially religious by something so essentially mundane as psychological testing? Beyond that, critics were convinced that even if testing were desirable, its attempted usage would do more harm than good. Testing might eliminate individuals whose spirituality could easily surmount their emotional difficulties, and Catholicism would lose fine priests and nuns.

But uncertain as he might have been, Father Bier had no thoughts of backing down. He believed that his work would fill a big hole in Catholic life if it were accepted. Years before, as a student at Catholic University in Washington, D.C., he had discussed with Father Thomas Verner Moore, the psychiatrist who became a priest, the problems of why people leave the religious life after they have given it their best years. No one really knew why they left, because their excuses were taken at their face value. As Fathers Bier and Moore saw it, the problem was to find out about these and other emotionally disturbed people *before* they began their studies.

The two men reached their conclusions just as new techniques of psychological testing became available. It was then that Father Bier conceived the idea of developing a special battery of tests for the religious vocation. The five years since he came to Fordham had largely been devoted to that project. This day in July was the public unveiling of his ideas.

The audience listened carefully as Father Bier posed his question: "How can we know in a given case that God calls? How can it be determined that the vocation is real and not illusory, genuine and not deceptive?"

Father Bier reviewed the contribution grace can make in a decision to enter the religious state. "You have not chosen me, but I have chosen you," he quoted from the Scriptures. "This is the essence of religious vocation, and it is clearly its supernatural aspect."

But then the psychologist-priest suggested that there were more considerations than the purely spiritual. "Human motivation, we know now, is a much more complex affair than was previously suspected. Our motives are seldom simple, and seldom single. Conscious motives can sometimes serve as a cloak for hidden and undetected tendencies."

To make his point Father Bier described a situation in which a young girl wanted to consecrate her virginity to God because she found "things of the flesh repugnant." The spiritual director questioning her learned that she found marriage abhorrent. What was his proper course?

"I can conceive of a director telling such a young girl to thank God that she feels that way, because she is thus freed from many temptations against chastity. Yet such advice, I think, would be highly questionable. It is true, of course, that such a person would have little or no difficulty with the material observance of chastity, but absence of sin or conflict is not a proof of virtue.

"It is God's plan that sex should be attractive, not repugnant, and it is clear from the words of Christ . . . and of St. Paul that the invitation to the counsels implies a sacrifice."

His audience's attention was undivided as Father Bier said firmly: "The girl who finds sex repugnant has no sacrifice to make in dedicating her virginity to God."

There was a further consideration to a case of this nature, he declared. Suppose, after years of religious life initiated by a psychic inhibition toward sex, this psychological twist suddenly straightened out. The woman might be defenseless against a passion whose existence she had never suspected. "Could it not be," said the priest, "that something similar to this is the explanation of some of those particularly puzzling defections after years in religion?"

He stressed that "the masters of the spiritual life" had always acknowledged the possibility of self-deception in service to God. Psychology, he insisted, could now confirm this intuitive estimate by showing that what externally passes for virtue may actually be no more than a cover up for some form of psychological problem:

Natural submissiveness and deep-seated inferiority could easily pass for humility.

Overconscientious strivings for perfection could be no more than psychological defenses against fear of criticism, inability to tolerate failure, and unconscious fear of the world.

Genuine apostolic zeal could easily be confused with paranoid discontent.

He warned:

"It would surely be excessive always to question our conscious motives and to see in them nothing but disguises for hidden tendencies, but it must also be acknowledged that conscious motives are sometimes deceptive, and that the dominant motives for our actions are not always the ones which consciously move us."

In his conclusion, Father Bier argued that religious life was so unusual and its demands so severe that extraordinarily stable persons were desirable. Tests should be given the candidates, and any doubts should be resolved *against them.* In cases of this nature it would not do anyone any good to take a chance.

There was an instant between the end of his speech and the beginning of the reaction. As Father Bier recalled later, it was "overwhelming." The audience of nuns, brothers, and priests he had figured to offend gave him an ovation.

That was his first surprise. A few months later came a second. *Review for Religious,* a publication for priests, decided to reprint Father Bier's lecture in the full expectation that many subscriptions would be lost as a result. Instead, the issue sold out.

Yet another surprise awaited. Father Bier, who had never before been in demand as a speaker, suddenly found himself with more requests than he could fulfill.

In United States seminaries, the principle of screening candidates for religious life, of which Father Bier was a singular pioneer, has in just one decade advanced from the exception to the rule. Today all but a few of the leading Protestant and Jewish seminaries, and most of the Catholic seminaries run by Jesuits, engage in some form of preadmission screening. Some groups of nuns have also taken to the procedure. The use of screening by Catholics would unquestionably be wider still if enough suitable personnel could be found to interpret the tests. The Catholic religious life, having a monastic quality that the other two lack, it is understandable that even Father Bier wants priest-psychologists, wherever possible, giving the tests. He says: "No one can

understand the demands of the life so well as a man who's
lived it."

With the Protestants and Jews, of course, no such restriction applies, and these groups are content to "farm out"
their screening programs to psychologists and psychiatrists.
Indeed, the Protestant participation in screening programs
grew so widespread that by 1953, according to a survey of
the National Council of the Churches of Christ in the U.S.A.,
some fifty distinct tests were being used by seminaries
throughout the country.

Today the use of screening techniques is considered so
important by the Protestants that they have even instituted
a program to test the tests. Thirteen denominations are
cooperating in an extensive analysis undertaken by the redoubtable Educational Testing Service of Princeton, New
Jersey, to which many colleges and industries turn for
methods to measure the intelligence or adeptness of prospects. The service intends to evaluate the tests by contrasting the predictions they made about what sort of ministers
candidates would be with the actual records they made in
later years in the ministry.

Underlying the effort of the clergy to find ways to eliminate psychologically unsuitable candidates from their seminaries are several conclusions.

Foremost is the realization that psychological conflict is
one of the characteristics of mid-twentieth-century life in the
United States. Our 650,000 mental-hospital patients equal
the number of all other hospital patients combined. One out
of every twelve children born today will need to go to a
mental hospital at some point in his life. According to the
National Association for Mental Health, 9,000,000 Americans are suffering from some form of mental or emotional
disorder. Three million men, one fifth of all those inducted,
were lost to the armed forces during World War II for

psychiatric reasons. Says Father Bier: "It seems nothing short of unrealistic to think that psychological difficulties will not also create a genuine problem in terms of admission to religious life."

A second major reason for the increased popularity of screening tests stems from the flat-footed admission by the clergy that the religious life has a tremendous appeal for emotionally troubled people. A classic study in this regard was made in 1935 by Father Moore, the psychiatrist cum priest. He found first of all that the rate of insanity for cloistered sisters—1,034 per 100,000 population—was almost twice that of the population at large, whose ratio was 595 per 100,000. The rate for priests was 446; while seemingly lower, it becomes higher the moment an adjustment is made for syphilitic types of insanity, which are almost completely absent among priests. If this factor were eliminated from the figures for the general population, the rate of insanity for priests would rise above that for the population at large.

The principal reason for the higher incidence of insanity, in the opinion of Father Moore, is the fascination exercised by the seclusion and retirement of religious life upon pre-psychotic personalities. The unwillingness of the preschizo-phrenic to mix with the world can pass for a desire for spiritual retreat, just as the insecurity of the neurotic draws him to the refuge of religious life, where he is sheltered from the demands that are made on him in ordinary life, and which he is unable to face.

A third reason why psychological testing of candidates has become so popular is that the clergy, especially the Catholics, have realized that the demands on them are different from the demands on most other people.

Speaking both as a psychologist and a priest, Father Bier suggests that spiritual writers who describe religious life as "martyrdom" are not far from the truth. "The vows of religion," says the priest, "involve the surrender of the three most basic natural rights: the right to possess, the right to marry, and the right to reasonable self-autonomy. In taking his vows, the religious freely renounces the exercise of these basic rights, but he does not change thereby his human nature which continues to clamor for these things. Can one doubt the reality of the psychological struggle—a lifetime struggle—between religious ideals and human wants, and can one doubt that the cumulative effect of such an enduring struggle deserves to be called a martyrdom? It seems self-evident that an applicant who has distinctly less than the average amount of psychological stability and maturity is ill-advised to embrace a life whose psychological demands are considerably more than average."

While Father Bier has obviously been speaking of Catholic religious life, his feelings about the desired emotional background of candidates for religious life are in accord with many Protestant and Jewish counselors with whom he has exchanged information.

Among these people it is generally held that under ideal circumstances an aspirant for a religious life should come not only from a religious home, but also a psychologically stable environment. "Homes in which turmoil, tension, bickering, and quarreling are the rule, and even more the broken home; homes where a parent is alcoholic or criminal or psychotic; homes where the parents are deeply unhappy and ill-suited to each other—these are not generally the homes from which psychologically suitable applicants come," says Father Bier.

But a product of any of these unfortunate environments looking for some way to extricate himself might readily see in religious life a haven that would give him the opposite of the turmoil he has known. While this is good for the individual, it is probably bad for religion, because the individual's past could not have avoided affecting him adversely, and the risk that he will make a bad clergyman is high. If he has individual problems, he is probably going to manipulate religion for his own uses. Says Father Bier: "An unfavorable home environment does not, *ipso facto*, preclude the vocation of an applicant . . . but it does make very careful individual examination a clear prerequisite."

If examining a candidate for the religious life is desirable, therefore, how do you go about it? To a certain extent, just as you examine any applicant for a job. You look into his history, because his past record is the best indication of his future course. You determine his physical health, because religious life can be even more demanding physically than an ordinary vocation. You look into his school work for a sign of any marked slumps, because they would indicate personal problems or the beginning, in some cases, of schizophrenia.

Above all, you look for unusual psychological behavior. Is the candidate peculiar—vastly different from others? Suspicious? Unsociable? Does he make friends? What does he do in idle hours? Says Father Bier: "We would be on the lookout for evidence of a *shut-in type of personality,* because of the fascination exercised by the seclusion of religious life upon such an individual."

Does he mope, sulk, or pout? Does he give up easily when things don't go his way? When does he get angry, and how does he act when he does? "Persons who are irritable and bad-tempered are not good prospects for the priesthood or religious life," notes the priest-psychologist. "Irritability when joined to a shut-in type of personality may be a sign of schizophrenia, and when joined to unsociability may be a sign of mania." He adds:

"Even though such individuals never suffer a mental break, they are likely to be troublesome members of a religious community, and as parish priests they have all kinds of difficulties with members of their congregations."

What sort of test will produce the results by which a sensible judgment can be made? In the case of Catholics, it was Father Bier's conclusion that the tests, while basically similar to personality tests, have to relate to the unusual life for which the candidate was intended. For example, a personality inventory designed to test marriage aptitude would obviously not do for aspirants to a celibate life.

It was for this reason that Father Bier spent years designing his own series of tests. Basically, they are intended to give information about significant relationships the candidate has had in his lifetime. While the tests are lengthy and elaborate, a few simple illustrations should explain their direction.

One of the most important prerequisites to training for Catholic religious life is that of obedience. Usually the presence of this quality in any young man can be determined if something is known about his relationship with his father. If it was a satisfactory relationship, it can be assumed that the candidate understands the need to obey his elders. Therefore, when he is examined for the priesthood, the young man is asked to fill in sentences that reflect his own situation.

One sentence begins simply: "My father . . ." If, as has often happened, the answer is "hardly ever speaks civilly to me," the examiner learns a good deal about the candidate's attitude toward obedience.

Another sentence begins, "My father and I . . ." Here frequent suspicious responses are "never speak to one another" or "don't understand one another" or "do not think alike." If, on the other hand, a candidate writes "My father and I . . . are wonderful pals," he has probably enjoyed a healthy relationship.

On the basis of these tests 10 per cent of all candidates are eliminated as bad psychological risks. Another 10 per cent are examined much more closely, usually by psychiatrists.

The things a psychiatrist looks for and finds can be illustrated by the work of Dr. Gotthard Booth of New York City who since 1949 has examined more than three hundred and fifty candidates for the Protestant Episcopal Church. Most of the candidates were first-year students at General Theological Seminary in New York and postulants of the diocese of Newark. Dr. Booth recently summarized his findings in a paper published by the Academy of Religion and Mental Health.

He notes that only infrequently are candidates for the ministry truly sick and can be screened out on the basis of serious pathology. His examination attempts to evaluate the candidates' strengths and weaknesses in personality structure, and to learn about the "problems of personal life which the candidate has not faced already in the past, such as marriage." Says Dr. Booth:

"In the ideal case the candidate would be attracted purely by the ideal aims of the Church, but in reality all candidates are influenced in varying degrees by nonspiritual needs for which the Episcopal ministry holds out satisfaction."

Any reasonable balance between the ideal and the actual is perfectly admissible, the psychiatrist notes, but certain candidates want the actual far more than the ideal.

Some, for example, are seeking conspicuous social dignity to overcome feelings of inferiority in their childhood. Others are looking for security "in my father's house" because they never got it from their actual father at home.

A third factor frequently driving young men into the church, says Dr. Booth, is homosexuality, often of a kind the candidate never suspects. He is seeking some form of "sublimated satisfaction" in the church, as well as an excuse for not marrying.

Finally, a man may be driven to the church to seek the emotional and aesthetic experiences of its religious services, for, as Dr. Booth points out, our culture makes such experiences available to very few men in normal settings.

One very strong conclusion emerged from Dr. Booth's nine years of testing: There were twice as many "conformists" as there were "individualists" among the Episcopal candidates. The conformists are content to subordinate their own values to those of the church. Furthermore, they are able to use the clerical setting as a stabilizing and directive force that compensates for their other limitations, Dr. Booth concludes. "One may say that for some the clerical dress provides a portable sanitarium . . . in which the individual accomplishes constructive work of which he would be incapable in a worldly setting."

The tests employed by Dr. Booth are threefold. The first is a written self-evaluation. The second is a series of four "projective personality" tests. The third is an interview with the psychiatrist himself.

It is in the second area that Dr. Booth makes considerable use of one of the most celebrated of all personality-measuring devices, the Rorschach ink-blot test. Conceived by the Swiss psychiatrist-neurologist Hermann Rorschach, this technique involves the presentation of a series of cards to an individual being examined. On the cards are meaningless blobs of ink. The patterns the individual sees in the ink blobs accurately reflect his own life patterns, and the effect of events on his personality.

For example, on the very first card one candidate said he saw what looked like "a battered piece of tin." Another said he saw a "worm-eaten leaf." A third said he saw a "badly beaten up butterfly." All three had gone through rough childhoods and were clearly showing that their lives as a result were "excessively handicapped," Dr. Booth judged.

Six candidates he saw revealed a preoccupation with face-saving. They wanted the church, Dr. Booth concluded, as a means of escaping some worldly reality they were unable to confront and anxious to find an excuse for not confronting. His evidence: All six saw masks and animal heads in the ink blots—which symbolically stood for devices to cover, i.e., save their own faces.

One type of card was especially revealing. It "trapped" a number of candidates who had not built up an adequate system of ego defenses during their early years. The cards, deliberately forbidding in design, would be viewed by a normal person as a threat of "disintegration under aggression." The normal response would be to reject these figures —for actually they do not pose a real threat—by seeing, instead, a more desirable pattern. A healthy individual who enjoys life will see some aspect of humor, such as the figure of a clown, or of happy, conventional behavior, such as people dancing, greeting, or toasting each other with drink. By rejecting the unfavorable picture for a more favorable one, the individual is proving that he can defend himself. Here is where ten "inadequate seminarians" came a cropper because they saw neither human nor animal figures, but instead some form of destruction. Five, for example, described a "bloody fight." Their ego defenses were all deficient.

No tests, no matter how exhaustive, can expect to succeed in religious vocational guidance to a perfect extent, and if there is one current running through all such programs it is this admission of fallibility. Examiners frequently acknowledge that while their tests can on many occasions save religion the embarrassment of an unstable clergyman, there is one intangible that can overcome all sorts of difficulties for psychologically disturbed individuals who want to be pastors. That intangible is "spirituality." Says Dr. Booth: "Spirituality, strong enough, can overcome all defects."

Even those who are involved in the training of clergymen for pastoral counseling duties worry that tests can be carried too far. Rabbi Robert Katz of Hebrew Union College points out that screening, while admittedly doing good, might eliminate exceptional individuals whose religious qualities are sufficiently profound to overcome questionable psychological qualities.

Father Bier also makes note of the spiritual factors involved in evaluating an individual for religious work. ". . . Psychological testing is finished, its work complete, its contribution made, when it has ascertained the facts. . . . It then becomes the superior's responsibility to act upon the facts as seems best. . . . A prudent superior will not come to a decision of course without taking the matter to prayer."

But even though the contribution be forever less than complete, even though mistakes be made, there is no doubt that the psychological testing of candidates has already raised the caliber of the religious fraternity by protecting it from the encroachment of undesirables. By their ever increasing patronage, religious leaders indicate that the inadequacies and injustices are as nothing compared to the virtues.

And at least one man is emphatic in his conviction that after spiritual and psychological factors have both been considered any and all doubts as to the suitability of an applicant for a life in religion be resolved against him—for his own sake, certainly, but even more for the people whose religion he would obscure. Says Father Bier, who helped start the whole program:

"In God's providence we shall always have enough difficult members of the community to make religious life a source of virtue and sanctification, but it seems quite another thing knowingly to contribute to the difficulties of religious life by admitting psychologically unsuitable persons . . .

"One such person can be a thorn in the side of an entire community, as experience well attests."

11.

THE HIT-AND-RUN PROFESSOR OF RELIGION AND HEALTH
or
"Mrs. Westberg, What Happened to Your Boy?"

As THE young doctor in the long white coat entered the hospital conference room he spotted a tape recorder. Immediately he turned to the man in charge and said, "Are you sure nobody's going to hear this?"

Assured that nobody (meaning his colleagues) would, the doctor slid into a chair at the side of the long conference table. He slid way down, as far as he could, into a position that appeared to match his mood. For the doctor, at that moment, had all the looks of an uncomfortable man. He was the only scientist in a room full of professional religionists.

For days he had hedged about attending this conference of divinity students from the University of Chicago. But the meeting had been unavoidable, for this was the university's hospital and he and the students had one common concern, an old and nervous man.

On admission to the hospital, the old man had become a patient of the doctor, but from the moment, on the twelfth day of his confinement, when he had asked to see a chaplain, he had become a case for the divinity students as well. For they were enrolled in a course whose very title might make a scientist shudder. It was called "Religion and Medicine."

Larger forces had been at work to make this meeting of science and religion inevitable. Doctors, as a general rule, were becoming markedly less critical of religion. In New York City, an Episcopal minister had just presented his seventeenth psychiatrist in eight months for confirmation. At the Menninger Foundation in Kansas, residents in psychiatry were studying religious symbols and other aspects of formal belief they were likely to encounter in their practice; the course, taught by chaplains, was required. The American Psychiatric Association had recently established a committee on religion and psychiatry, with Dr. Earl Loomis as its chairman. And at hospitals and seminaries the country over doctors and clergy were meeting as never before to discuss their mutual concern, man.

The most succinct explanation for this activity had come from a man who, having devoted his life to the movement, had earned the respect of both its elements. "Psychiatry," wrote Theologian David E. Roberts, "is just waking up to the fact that . . . it must exercise practical and religious functions which put it on the side of 'sound religion' instead of 'no religion.' " [1] For doctors were discovering that not only must they have an understanding of religion to understand religious patients; they required a sound philosophy of their own to support patients whose neurotic views they destroyed.

Out of all this foment had emerged a significant by-product that was gladdening the hearts of religion and psychiatry alike. That by-product was a revitalized hospital chaplaincy.

The contempt that many doctors had reserved for chaplains in the past had been not only astounding for its vehemence, but to some extent deserved. For years the chaplaincy had

[1] *The Church and Mental Health*, p. 21.

been viewed by many members of the clerical fraternity as the Siberia of American religious life. Hospitals, in some cases, had developed into convenient dumping grounds for used-up pastors. Chaplains' duties were too often more like those of a hostess than a man of God. Performances were largely measured not by the understanding and support chaplains could offer patients in distress, but by the amounts of literature they could distribute each month.

Much of this had changed. With an added understanding of what makes people sick, brought on in some cases by the mere experience of living in the age of psychology, and in others by an admission that they were not effectively reaching their people, religious groups had come to realize that vigorous, educated clergymen, not superannuated ones, belonged in hospitals. As the Reverend Wayne Oates put it: "There is no doubt that there are religious people in hospitals, and they need religious help." If the religious groups were to support their members in any truly authentic fashion, they had to get their young clergymen trained to a scientific understanding of the emotions in people that produce problems.

The response to this new view had been stunning. In ever increasing numbers seminaries and other religious institutions were offering courses in clinical training, and young clergymen were invading the hospitals for a meaningful association with people in distress. Out of this activity had come not only better counselors, but better chaplains, too.

Again the most direct analysis of what was happening came from David E. Roberts. Speaking for his own faith, he might, with modification, have included the other two: "The Protestant pastorate is just waking up to the fact that contemporary psychotherapy, along with perennial Christian resources, may revitalize the healing function of the Church and throw fresh light upon traditional doctrine." [2]

2 *Op. cit.,* p. 21.

Thus there were many developments from which the uneasy young doctor in the hospital conference room might have taken heart. But even had he not been aware that many older doctors, particularly psychiatrists, were coming to a new appreciation of religion, even had he not been aware of the rebirth of a sound chaplaincy within his own short lifetime, he was, at this moment, in the best possible position to figure out what was happening for himself. For the man at whose side he sat, the man whose class he had agreed to assist, was the most striking embodiment of both developments in the country today.

Young and thorough, quiet yet bold, Lutheran Minister Granger Westberg is as remarkable in his world as a Jewish United States president would be in his. He is the first clergyman ever to serve as a professor at a school of medicine. Though he has had to fight for respect, he is today greatly admired by practitioners of both religion and psychiatry, the two approaches to salvation that entwine his life.

His distinction developed by accident. He had been the pastor of St. John's Lutheran Church in Bloomington, Illinois, for five years after his ordination when he was asked one day to substitute for a week as chaplain of the Augustana Lutheran Hospital in Chicago. "That," he recalls, "was a week I'll never forget."

The doctors were so surprised to see a young chaplain that at first they refused to take him seriously. "What are you doing here?" one of them scoffed. "You get in trouble?" Said another: "Don't you know the average age of chaplains is seventy-seven?"

But when young Westberg, an enthusiastic man, showed a real concern for their work, the doctors let him have it. "Why doesn't the Church take an interest in the patient in the bed?" they demanded. "Why does the Church put tired men in the hospitals? Why don't these men ever talk to anyone on a really deep level?"

Mr. Westberg was defenseless. The charges, he felt, were true. It was his experience that chaplains never did talk on deep levels, either because they no longer could, or because they never could. In a hospital setting they were about as essential as an appendix.

Not long thereafter the chaplains' committee of the hospital met to find a new man. The committee, of which Mr. Westberg was a member, proposed several candidates. Each candidate turned the committee down after first making it clear that he considered the very offer an insult of the most severe kind.

Finally, the committee found itself with no takers and no more candidates. It was at this point that Mr. Westberg, proving that his week as a chaplain had indeed been memorable, turned to his colleagues and uttered the words that changed his life. "Have you ever thought of me?"

He shocked them, but he got the assignment. Knowing of the popular belief that the title of "minister" was reserved for those clergymen who had a parish, he was not surprised at what followed. Another minister said to him, "So you've left the ministry." A friend of his mother inquired, "Mrs. Westberg, what happened to your boy?" Another consoled her, "Don't worry. He'll get a parish again."

She was wrong. He never did. He studied psychology and psychiatric techniques. He studied the movements of doctors and nurses, trying to see how a religious professional could abet their work. Above all, he tried to find for himself the relation of religion to people in distress.

On the preventive side of emotional illness he introduced a premarital counseling clinic. He began a clinical training course for pastors and theological students. He served as an instructor at the Chicago Lutheran Theological Seminary and McCormick Theological Seminary, carrying the message that a chaplain was vital to the needs of religion and its people. He became the second president of the American Protestants' Hospital Chaplains' Association in 1946. In 1952 he resigned from Augustana to accept an appointment as chaplain of the University of Chicago clinics which, in terms of impact, is about like moving from the State House to Congress, and to serve as associate professor of pastoral care at the Federated Theological Faculty at the university. On June 1, 1956, Granger Westberg became associate professor of Religion and Health with a joint appointment on the Federated Theological Faculty and the Medical School Faculty of the University of Chicago. He and the institution of the chaplaincy had arrived.

Because many doctors were displeased by the development, Mr. Westberg met considerable initial resistance. The break came when the heads of three departments of the medical school sat in on a few of his classes to see for themselves. Afterward they invited him to send his divinity students on the rounds with the doctors.

Today not only does Mr. Westberg teach divinity students, he also gives an introductory course in religion to freshman medical students. His function has so captured the fancy of other medical schools that he receives invitations by the score to lecture at campuses throughout the country. At one point, when he realized that he was spending several weeks of the year away from his own job, Mr. Westberg felt compelled to apologize to the head of the medical school. The response not only encouraged him; it gave him possession of a new and unusual sobriquet. "Don't worry," said his superior, "you'll be my hit-and-run professor of religion and health."

As might be expected from his experience, Professor Westberg feels a profound debt to science. "I came to an appreciation of religion through psychiatry," he remarked recently. "Psychiatry showed us that we were really superficial. Before a man said, 'I believe in the Lord Jesus Christ' and the minister would ask him, 'Are you saved?' and he'd say 'Yes, I'm saved.' And then he'd go out and yield to temptation and really get screwed up. So then he'd come back and say, 'There are times, Reverend, when I have a bad feeling for my wife,' and the Reverend would say, 'Well, but you feel good about her, too, don't you?' and the man would say, 'Well, yes, sometimes I do.' And the Reverend would say, 'Well, now, that's what I like to hear. Fine. Fine. The Lord bless you. Fine. Fine, fine. That's fine, fine.'

"Today when a man comes in for a private talk you know he's got something bothering him. So when he says he's felt good about his wife we say, 'All week long?' "

Not only the healing resources of the Church, but its very orientation has been restored by new insights, Professor Westberg believes. "Psychiatry has reminded the Church of the unquestionable optimism the Christian faith has regarding man's potential self. In practice we'd been emphasizing too much the sinful nature of man."

It is this eclectic viewpoint that has enabled Professor Westberg to achieve the success he has with doctors. He says: "As I judge the doctors—especially the GP's—they're ready for a little religion. My aim is to have the doctor look at religion as a factor in the health process. It doesn't mean a man is cured because he's no longer throwing up."

And it was precisely this situation with which Professor Westberg was dealing this day. The young doctor had found nothing radically wrong with the old man who was to be the subject of the class's concern, and was prepared, therefore, to discharge him. The procedure was perfectly in order, but in Professor Westberg's terms it was completely in-

adequate to the situation. For the old man was not emotionally well.

To get his point across would not be easy. There is a
common, innate, and perfectly explainable hostility to religion among many young doctors. Enthralled with their own
new understanding of the healing power of medicine, they
are naturally skeptical of medication with prayer. By function dealers in fact, they instinctively distrust faith. Since
evidence makes up their minds, they are hostile to a system
that appears to them to make up evidence.

Furthermore, there is very little public awareness today
of the great distance religion has put between itself and
the giddy, ineffectual moralistic movement that dominated—
and alienated—many religious groups a generation ago. A
doctor, just like anyone else relying on memory rather than
recent observation, could remember religion as boundlessly
optimistic and totally unrealistic.

But even the young doctor who had not wanted to become
involved with the divinity students should have seen enough
realism this day to make him realize that things were different
now. These divinity students were as far removed from
moralistic thought as a mongrel from best-of-breed.

For months they had been toughening up on some demanding cases. Twice, for example, they had deeply explored the chaplain's relationship to people who were dying.
One woman in her forties, a mother of three, was slowly being
consumed by a cancer that had spread from her breast through
her body. Flitting between a desire to face death with courage and another to avoid the truth about her illness, she
had posed grave questions for the young theologians. How
do they deal with her demand to know why God's plan
should include her personal calamity? And what do they tell
her about her illness? Has a dying patient a right to know
the truth? The chaplain in charge had concluded that al-

though he risked being attacked as "morbid and a threat to morale," he was for telling the truth "so that the person involved may have an opportunity to grow to that higher level of human dignity and fulfillment made possible in crises."

The second case had seemed even more tragic, because the woman involved, also the mother of three, was only twenty-eight. Bright, poised, college-educated, she had displayed extraordinary maturity and was able to discuss not only her oncoming death, a result of Hodgkin's disease, but her husband's eventual remarriage. Her courage was not her complete story, however. The Reverend Alan Richardson, a member of Professor Westberg's staff, had observed that she vacillated between periods of acceptance and others of morosely denying her fate. Her more positive side, he felt, was an expression of what she believed would be acceptable to the minister. Very sick people "talk about the things they feel the minister wants to hear," Mr. Richardson had noted. Assuming the woman's attitude was not genuine, how, it was asked of the students, can religion create a realistic attitude toward death? Or is religion just a palliative? The answer, again, was an affirmation of realism. Said Mr. Richardson: "The minister must not accentuate the positive and eliminate the negative."

There was also the case of the big man with the racing heart, the pugnacious attitude, and the childhood in a broken home. Admitted to the hospital after several heart attacks, he could not accept the rest and quiet he needed to recover. He was too impulsive. Once he had run inside a tavern he happened to be passing to "clean up" on whoever had just bounced a customer. Another time he had seen a motorist run over a dog. Believing the accident could have been avoided, he had raced his own car ahead of the motorist, forced him to the curb, and urged him to fight. When he finally got to talking with the chaplain, he portrayed God as a watchdog always on the lookout for aggressors. He felt that God was always watching him, and that he was always in danger of trouble. To help himself, he would help God.

What, the divinity students were asked to decide, could they do about this man's neurotic concept of "Father"? An involved question, it hinged on their ability to make him see how his own emotional tendencies related to his identification with his father, who had been forced from his home in humiliation when the son was very young.

No doctor, regardless of his attitude toward religion, could fail to see that the problems taken up by the divinity students were every bit as significant in terms of well-being as was disease itself. Even so, none of the cases had quite the element of the one today, for none had directly confronted the concept of religious omniscience as did this one. No doctor, no matter how skeptical, could fail to admire the decision reached by the clergyman in the case of the elderly laborer who was being besieged by doubts he did not have the training to comprehend.

It was a "bag-lunch" conference. A dozen students were munching sandwiches and sipping from half-pint containers of milk. Just as the class got under way, one of the hospital's psychiatrists slipped in, sat down, and unwrapped an aromatic salami sandwich and a wedge of chocolate cake.

The diagnosis was brief. In a low voice the young doctor told the class that his patient was sixty-nine and worried about his bowels. He'd had a stroke several months before, suffering partial paralysis of his left side. An interesting feature of the stroke was that it had occurred in the same month that his wife had completed an unsuccessful therapy for an illness that would eventually claim her. "His wife's problems are significantly related to his," the doctor noted. But even though he knew the man was concerned about his health, the doctor had found no severe medical problems. His only course, therefore, was to order the patient sent home.

The chaplain's report produced a new dimension. After several false starts the sick man had asked for religious counsel. When the chaplain arrived, he was pacing the corridor and wringing his hands. He took the chaplain's arm and they walked to a lounge where they could converse in private.

There he broke down. "I'm not ready to go home," he pleaded. He became more and more nervous as the day of his discharge approached. He knew that the good news about his physical condition should have made him feel wonderful. But tears streamed down his face as he confessed that he felt more depressed than ever, and didn't know why. "God has been good to me," he cried, "so why should I have doubts and nervousness now?"

The case was a classic one. Few days pass in the lives of chaplains when they do not hear a sick man state his belief that God will take care of him. Usually he doesn't believe it at all. He's terrified, and often for a reason as classic as was this case. He is overcome by guilt.

The old man was not at all sure that God would be good to him, because he was not sure he had been good enough to God. He hadn't gone to church very often, nor had he given much to support its work. As he worried about death, he now found his religious life deficient. He had always thought of God as a stern judge; now he was terrified of judgment. He felt completely cut off from God, and he did not believe he could be forgiven for his sins.

What should religion do to help this man?

His pastor, who was present for the conference by invitation, had tried. Admitting that the doctors and chaplains had "learned in a few days what it took me five years to find out," he recalled hectic scenes in the man's home where, drinking quantities of coffee and pacing through the house, the man had confessed to baffling feelings of guilt. He would ask the pastor to read from the Bible, and particularly for those psalms characterized by considerable expression of guilt.

"I told him there is forgiveness available for our guilt," the pastor recalled.

But obviously it hadn't worked. Thus far his religion had not been able to help the old man in time of stress. The question was, could it? In his report Professor Westberg had noted the following:

"This is an example of a man who appears to be very friendly but is so tied in with his anxiety and depression that it appears clearly that he tends to use any available person for support."

Professor Westberg then raised a key question. "Is this an effort to so relate to others that he will not need to confront himself at some deeper level?" He pointed out that the patient's emotional stresses, largely undealt with, "are now emerging in ways which confuse and depress him."

To the class, Professor Westberg gave this warning: "Because of such a long experience of not having dealt with such emotions at any significant depth at all, such confrontation at this time is extremely difficult and perhaps dangerous."

In other words, *talking to this man about sin and forgiveness, about guilt and salvation, the very questions that preoccupy religion, might hurt this man, not help him.*

The psychiatrist, asked for his evaluation, confirmed the judgment. "If guilt is pretty deep-seated, an attempt to find solace in religion doesn't always work. If a man is to the point where he feels he's sinned so much God can't help him, seeing a chaplain may be helpful, and it may not.

"If you say he'll be forgiven, and nothing changes for him, he'll be worse."

The psychiatrist recommended some form of masculine striving, such as gardening, in which by prodding, digging, shoveling, and ultimately growing a product he would feel satisfactions not unlike those felt by a father. But under no circumstances was there to be any further attempt to arrive at a religious understanding of his plight.

"Any deep talk at this point might overcome him," the psychiatrist warned.

Twenty years ago the prescription for a man's salvation that excluded religion on the grounds that it would hinder, not help, would have been considered a blasphemy. To these future ministers, however, it made complete sense. The young doctor could hardly have asked for more.

12.

SIGMUND FREUD IN SUNDAY SCHOOL

I N Washington, D.C., recently, one of this country's top
government administrators happened to fall into a discussion with his twelve-year-old son about the boy's Sunday-
school program. What the son told him proved so disquieting
that the official immediately asked to see his study materials.
That perusal, in turn, so alarmed the official that the following Sunday he went to the church school itself to observe
a class firsthand. When the class ended, he sought out the
minister to express his great concern over the manner in
which Sunday-school instruction had deteriorated since he
was a boy.

Because the man and his opinion were of some consequence, the minister determined to make a major effort to explain what had happened. Not only did he argue for the new
program himself, but he summoned the best education minds
of his church to Washington from nearby cities for a dinner
meeting with the executive.

Just how successful the religious educators were in convincing the executive they were never quite certain; he
at least seemed reassured to a point where he thought of no
further protest. But there is at least one certain aspect to
the incident. It proves the contention of some Protestant

leaders that in churches where the psychiatric impact has been felt an adult enrolling his child at his religious alma mater would hardly recognize the old school.

The alumnus would find that where he as a child had often been relegated to the darkest corners, his own child would occupy the nicest room in the church.

He would find that where he had usually followed a rigidly scheduled lesson plan, his own child would be left pretty much to his own devices in discussing topics as he found them interesting.

He would find that the typically firm and didactic Sunday-school teacher who made him recite Scriptures had been supplanted by someone who seemed at least as concerned with his son as with the Bible. Where he had been pushed into belief, his child was to be led by the hand. Where he had been told, his son was to experience.

The cumulative result of these innovations has been a program that might well make uneasy any parent who, like the government administrator, had assumed that his child would get the same theological orientation he did, based on a literalistic interpretation of the Bible. Such a technique today is regarded by the Department of Religious Education of the National Council of the Churches of Christ as the poorest of form. In conferences and through publications the Council's experts stress to member denominations that the duty of the teacher is just what the minister's duty has come to be, to listen instead of preach, to draw out rather than inject.

In many respects the parent would be finding the same sort of improvements in facilities and teaching methods he would encounter if he were to return to his old first-grade classroom at public school. But there is a significant area in which the change is accountable to the same forces that have so drastically altered the lives of some clergymen and changed the character of what they preach.

The most decisive force of all was a concern among Prottestant educators with increasing evidence of their lack of effectiveness. Somewhere in the decade between 1936 and 1946 many of them had begun to admit that they had failed to win church members to a working belief in Christianity. The churchgoer, educators gloomily admitted, had learned creeds but not lived by them, memorized the Bible but seen nothing deep in it. A whole generation, as an Episcopal publication put it, had gone through Sunday school without "catching" Christianity.

There was nothing intuitive about these estimates; they were based on solid facts. The Presbyterians, for example, had noted as early as the late thirties that Sunday-school enrollment had been declining steadily, and that the circulation of its Westminster Departmental Graded Lessons had dropped significantly. In an effort to find out why, the church's publications division sent out a questionnaire. It received an almost incredible 43 per cent return, and the nature of the response showed why. The church's educational approach was attacked for its "pious sentimentalism," its "lack of content," and its "general impoverishment."

A few years later another decisive development occurred. Many clergymen who went into the service in World War II had an opportunity to see how their young church members put religion to use in meeting the tests of stress and change. What the clergy found shocked them. Few churchgoing soldiers had learned anything in Sunday schools; many had arrived at a distorted idea of religion; still others had become totally indifferent. Emerging from the war, one hundred Episcopal chaplains issued a biting formal indictment:

"We are appalled at the indifference of the American people to Christ and their ignorance of Christianity's basic teachings about God and man. . . . We are alarmed at the degree to which the young men and women of our own church, as we meet them in the armed forces, are uninstructed in the faith and unaware of its devotional, moral, and social implications."

What had caused this lack of communication? A frequent criticism from caustic church leaders themselves is that the Church has a way of lagging behind secular developments —and there were several instances to point to now. With the emancipation of women and the ascension of mothers to equal partnership in the home, the family had become less and less inclined to permit the father to rule unquestioned. In a sense what had happened to fathers had also happened to religion. Asserts Samuel Blizzard, the sociologist: "The old concept of a paternalistic, authoritarian Church fits very well in a paternalistic authoritarian society. But it is not pertinent in a democratic permissive society. The Church is no longer the dominant force in moving people." Yet by and large the Church had continued to act as though nothing had changed.

A second factor inhibiting the Church, according to observers, was a lack of realism in handling sex morals. In the period following popularization of Freud's theory of the libido, Victorian morality in the secular world had been all but swamped. People became less and less willing to be restricted in their inquiries as to what was right and wrong. If sex was such a powerful force, they wanted theology to take a fresh look at it in the light of today's best thinking. This, many clergymen themselves now admit, the Church was for a period unwilling to do.

A third factor that inhibited church effectiveness, and subsequently led to drastic revision of the Sunday-school teacher's role, was the discovery that experience rather than lecture induced effective learning. "We're much more aware of the importance of participation today," notes Mrs. Alice Goddard, a National Council expert on education. "I can tell you about God. Did you say, 'I understand'? If you did, then it's still my idea. But if you experience an awareness of God through yourself, through your dealings with other people, then you know God." The same goes for love, Mrs. Goddard contends. "Instead of talking of love with youth we realize we must give them an experience of love." In terms of the teaching approach the difference is basic.

One other factor, very much in evidence in the literature and statements of many educational veterans, is the same as that which resulted in a diminution of the moralistic preaching that was so evident in Protestant churches a few decades ago. It is the factor of recognition that psychiatry had given to the need for "an adequate self-concept." Says Mildred Magnuson, who heads the National Council's child education division, "A child couldn't get a sense of his own worth if a Sunday-school teacher was telling him he was sinful and guilty." Such a practice, prevalent ten and twenty years ago, was destined to lose popularity for still another reason. Like the clergy, teachers had learned from psychiatry that emphasis on wickedness, sinfulness, or condemnation could lead to injurious feelings of guilt.

That child is handicapped who feels "I am a worm in the dust" [the *International Journal of Religious Education* noted in a special issue in February 1955]. . . . Accordingly we should beware of fostering guilt where there is no reason for it. General statements regarding the sinful state of every person, and morbid concern over the breaking of rules, may have a blighting effect upon a sensitive child. Adults frequently seek to interpret God's will in terms of their own standards of right and wrong. In so doing they sometimes instill a sense of guilt and fear in a child which makes him outwardly conforming and religious but inwardly frightened, hurt, and rebellious.

Of course, Christian education must provide the clear moral guidance necessary for the integration and stability of the person. Such morality, however ... should not be based on innumerable rigid rules under which certain actions are always categorically right and other actions always categorically wrong.

Psychiatric insights, the article went on, have made religious teachers aware of the negative, destructive feelings in all people, and of the imperative need to deal sympathetically with these emotions.

Destructive behavior may have at its source, behind all the surface hostility, a deep craving for love. The child or youth (or adult for that matter) who is a constant source of distraction may be greatly in need of affection, recognition, attention. His behavior is symptomatic of his underlying needs.

This troubled individual's ability to control his undesirable conduct begins when the teacher shows him that he is accepted regardless of what his feelings may be, the article states. "When a person is angry or makes a mistake but all the while is understood, loved, and forgiven, he comes to sense the divine love that undergirds life and makes for secure Christian growth."

At least as significant as the content of the article was its sponsorship by the National Council of the Churches of Christ. The Council's many member denominations are completely autonomous, and nothing the Council does in any way alters their independence. Yet, like any association of separate but similarly inclined organizations, the Council has come to be an accurate reflection of the moods of its constituents, in so far as this is possible within the Protestant spectrum. But even more significant, the Council is the body to which most of the church groups look for resources beyond their own. The Council emphasis on a family approach to education finds its counterpart in many denominations, and Council-sponsored or guided symposia, clinics, and conferences on leadership, teaching, and related problems are well attended by the various faiths. The mood of the Council itself, therefore, is of supreme importance in attempting to read the current story of religion in the Sunday schools. Clearly the main character in this narrative has been depth psychology.

The admission was made by the Council in a report issued recently supporting proposed changes—the first in thirty years—in the well-known "Objectives of Christian Education" that govern the formulation of most Protestant church school curriculums. Said the report:

The leadership of Christian education has changed greatly since the present list of objectives was formulated, and there have been marked changes in the educational and theological "climate" in which Christian education takes place. Many new discoveries have been made about the nature of personality, the processes of growth, and the place of moral and spiritual values in personality development. The task of Christian education in the total life and work of the church is seen in a different perspective.

One direct result of the changing mood of religious educators has been a vastly more direct confrontation of sex instruction. William Genné, who heads the Family Life Department of the Council, is emphatic in contrasting the difference. "Thirty years ago sex education was simply nonexistent," he recalls. "We had, instead, a lot of judgmental preaching about sin as though it were solely a matter of willful choice." Spreading several pamphlets before him, he declared: "This material just wasn't in existence ten years ago."

In one of the pamphlets, *Sex Facts for Adolescents,* Mr. Genné, writing with his wife, discusses physical development, menstruation, fertilization, and the sexual urge itself. The treatment is straightforward, and the closest the authors get to what could be called a warning is a statement in which they liken the handling of a sexual urge to the handling of a powerful automobile.

A good driver knows that brakes are as essential as a motor to reach a destination. Indeed, the auto engineers built the brakes three times more powerful than the motor. Just as a car has its built-in brakes, so we must have our own built-in controls of the sex urge to help us toward our goal. If a driver skids out of control on a curve, he is finished. If we skid out of control at the first sexual urge, it is doubtful whether we will reach our goal of the fullest enjoyment of a home and family.

A fetching cover of a young man nuzzling a pretty girl in an off-the-shoulder gown sets the tone of another notable pamphlet called *Sex, Love, and Marriage,* also distributed by the Council. After examining the various forms of immature and mature love, the pamphlet, written by W. Clark Ellzey, says, "The taboos have been broken and the public press has flooded the country with partial knowledge about sex." Urging the reader to study sex thoroughly, the pamphlet goes on: "Sex is like fire. Take fire out of our modern civilization and you would wreck it. Let it get out of hand through ignorance or carelessness, and it is devastating in its destruction. . . .

"Sure the moralities need re-examining, but don't be so foolish that you pitch them out—hook, line, and sinker."

Discussing premarital adjustment, the pamphlet contends that "attitudes and feelings which accompany sex affairs outside marriage often work against the achievement of success in marriage. What is learned may have to be unlearned before even a start can be made toward a sexually healthy marriage." On these grounds experimentation with a prostitute should be avoided, because "she does not respond as a normal woman, and any man who expects similar response from his wife or treats his wife according to what he has learned from a prostitute might easily wreck this part of his relationship with his wife right from the start."

What is significant here is not only what the pamphlet states, but what it doesn't state. Not long ago, according to Mr. Genné, a far more likely approach would have been to specify that any user of a prostitute was a sinner. Here the argument is a practical one, and nothing is being said of sin.

A pamphlet called *The Challenge of the Kinsey Report,* by Richard E. Lentz, pretty well sums up the Council's outlook:

People now recognize that the sexual aspects of their life are God-created, too. The purposes of God in creation are revealed to a considerable extent in the yearnings of men. Dogma alone will not satisfy modern men and women in dealing with their sexual yearnings. . . .

At present the Church, except in a few isolated cases, is unprepared to help them. Partly by the Kinsey report, but mostly by the needs of men, the best minds of the Church need to be challenged to this search for the will of God.

Another significant measure of how far into church life the discoveries of depth psychology have gone is the use educators are making of the revelation that children view God as a "father image." A widely distributed Council pamphlet, *How a Child's Idea of God Develops,* reflects the concern of religious leaders with discoveries that parents, and ministers themselves at times, have given children a distorted notion of God. Says the pamphlet: "It must be admitted that much of what we have given to children in the name of the Christian religion has not led to a helpful fellowship with God . . . often the very activity which we carry on in an effort to build up an awareness of God gives the child the wrong *idea* of God."

To illustrate, the pamphlet tells of a seven-year-old child who one day in some distress asked an adult friend, "Will God knock you dead with a bolt of lightning if you steal an apple?" He and a playmate, it developed, had stolen an apple from a neighborhood grocer. A third youngster had assured them that they would be found dead in their beds the following morning, because God destroyed anyone who stole. How did he know? His aunt had told him that the Bible said so.

In another instance an exasperated mother assured her eight-year-old daughter that God would punish her for her disobedience. The following day her beloved baby sister died suddenly. Certain that this was God's promised punishment, she was inconsolable.

The pamphlet cited a survey made among several thousand school children. They were asked whether a child who lied would be punished even if his fib was undiscovered. "A great majority of the answers," says the pamphlet, "reveal very anti-Christian ideas of God." Some of them: "We may get run over by an accident, but God has made the accident." "One way God could punish him is to make him always afraid and very unlucky." "God might let his house be struck by lightning or something fall on him and kill him."

It is strange and humiliating to think that children build their thoughts of God not infrequently upon our poor human imperfections [the pamphlet explains]. There are parents who promise what they have no thought of giving ... who punish today for that same conduct at which they laughed yesterday, who shower affection when they are happy themselves but scold without reason when they are disturbed. There are those who lie before a child in order to save train fare and then punish the child severely for lying to escape the consequences of an accident. In such a family the child lives in moral confusion and it is well-nigh impossible for him to develop an idea of the universe that is orderly, purposeful, intelligent, and reliable.

The pamphlet deplores the opposite tendency, as well, to smother children in affection and not allow them to be accountable for their errors. "The child in such a family will have difficulty in understanding that God expects his children to work with him to make his world beautiful and fruitful and strong."

"But," says the pamphlet, "there are more direct religious teachings which affect the child's idea of God." Echoing psychiatric theory down the line, it declares:

. . . as a result of some unwise teaching, some careless remark, the child comes to feel that God is not so loving as his mother, nor so just as his father, nor so wise as his teacher. A strange phenomenon which is often observed is that of a parent who tells his child that God will send dire punishments which the parent himself would not think of inflicting. Through the telling of certain stories in the Old Testament not well adapted to the stage of maturity of young children . . . through the repetition of some formula regarding God, through the singing of an unworthy hymn, the child is actually learning to hate God. . . .

One counterforce alone can bring children to a proper understanding of God, the pamphlet concludes. "Our children . . . must become aware of the thought and the love and the purpose of God as these are revealed to them in the world in which they are living."

While the changes under way in the National Council's educational approach are mirrored in the denominations in varying degrees, not every denomination is willing to acknowledge that psychiatry has played a significant role in the reorientation. An interesting comparison in this regard is that between the Presbyterians and the Episcopalians. Both

groups were impelled to act as a consequence of a dramatic
clamor from their ranks. Both made prolonged preparations
to revise their programs and textbooks, holding conferences,
hiring and training large staffs. Both created programs based
on the involvement of the entire family. Theologically, both
insisted on the emphasis of a number of religious principles
that for years had been obscured: that God accepts you for
what you are, that sin is "estrangement from God," not deviation from rules, and that the Bible is not a source for
"bibliolatry," a set of inflexible modes of human conduct,
but instead a well of deep, philosophical ideas of man's relationship to his universe.

Officials of the Board of Christian Education of the Presbyterian Church freely acknowledge the use they are making
of psychiatrists and psychologically oriented editors in their
current work. In recalling the inception of the revision, however, they agree only that psychiatry might have influenced
the direction of the revision "by osmosis," but they insist
that the influence was not direct.

The Episcopal attitude is the complete reverse. Theirs was
a calculated and open effort to bring the best insights of
psychiatry to religious education. The Reverend John Heuss,
who directed the initial program of revision, deliberately
surrounded himself with a psychiatrically oriented board of
directors, including one pastoral counseling expert in whom
many Episcopalians take great pride, Reuel L. Howe. Had
psychiatry changed any of their religious viewpoints? One
close observer bluntly states:

"I don't know whether it can be said for a lot of people,
but by George it can be said for a lot of people on that
board."

The key word, it must be stressed, is "changed" and
not "invented." If the Council's view that children become
aware of the love of God through "the world in which they

are living" is given even a perfunctory examination, it can still be seen that there is nothing inventive about the thoughts therein. The sentence is a summation of "good religion" by which many religious professionals have always lived and taught. It must be emphasized again that to give psychiatry credit for *inventing* the thought would be silliness in the extreme.

Clearly, however, psychiatry proved itself a catalyst in restoring many religionists to a more precise and useful faith—and it is the professionals themselves who make this analysis. "There's always been an *insightful* minority acting this way," says Alice Goddard of the National Council. "Now it's spread to a majority of the people who influence thought."

13.

DISSENTS

THE suggestion that psychiatry has affected religion in significant ways in the last thirty years in this country meets in many quarters today with immediate acceptance. In many others, however, it does not, and the vehement reactions are these:

That psychiatry has not affected religion at all.

That psychiatry is being suggested as the sole cause of a change that was really the result of a combination of factors.

That an acceptance of the thesis that certain religious attitudes have changed from bad to good inevitably implies that all religious attitudes were bad to begin with.

That religion, in embracing psychiatry, has neglected theology and as much as admitted that theology was bankrupt.

That religion, in applying psychiatric insights and techniques, is practicing medicine without a license.

A denial that the contact with psychiatry has had any effect on religion can only be based either on a lack of information or on a desire to avoid the trouble that must surely follow any assertion that science is "tampering" with religion. It may have been the latter thought that the retiring president of the American Psychiatric Association, Dr. Francis J. Braceland, of Hartford, Connecticut, had in mind when he restated in his 1957 farewell address a warning he had expressed privately a year before in specific reference to the suggestion that psychiatry has affected religious attitudes.

"If psychiatry is to take its proper place in the science of man, it must be aware of its limitations and realize that it is only a part of this science, an important but a small part in so far as the general knowledge of man is concerned. To forget this is to run the danger of scientific imperialism. By this term I mean to indicate the tendency, encountered regularly in the history of knowledge, to credit a special discipline with universal significance. The final result of such enthronement is always the catastrophic dethronement of the apparently supreme branch of knowledge."

To begin with, psychiatry neither seduced nor forced itself upon religion. The evidence indicates quite clearly that the approach was made from the other direction, that a sizable, influential, and intelligent group of theologians, finding themselves alive in the age of psychology, did the obvious thing. They explored the new knowledge for insights they could apply to their own situation. It was they who found in psychiatry "universal significance."

That psychology and psychiatry were the only sciences from which religion gained insights in this century is of course not true. Much has been learned not only sociologically but cosmologically, and resilient bodies within religion have reacted admirably in their attempts to interpret man's spiritual place in an expanding universe. Progress would have been made even had the unconscious remained a mystery. But the significant point here is the one made by religionists themselves: psychiatry produced the high drama that implemented the high ideals as never before.

"The Renaissance, the Enlightenment, the Liberal Movement of the nineteenth and twentieth centuries all contributed to the change," says Sarah Lawrence College's Dr. Maurice Friedman, the religious philosopher and historian. "But these movements could only set ideals aglimmering. Men knew what religion should be. But the ideals remained on a conscious abstract or sentimental level, and therefore did not become operational. Men did not accept these things in practice. With psychiatry the ideals were able to become concrete, because psychiatry deals with specific men in their full dynamics. Psychiatry created the decisive opening needed to get the ideals across."

It would be a misrepresentation to suggest that psychiatry has gotten these ideals across to every churchgoer, and that the movement toward a religion allied with psychiatry is thus the only motion discernible within religion today. Certainly a case can be made, often with factual justification, that religion's newest, most exciting, and fastest-growing trend is toward the "psychological church." Clergymen smitten by possibilities inherent in the religion-psychiatry alliance point out that at the rate ministers are being trained in depth insights, nearly half the churches and synagogues in the United States will have come under this new influence within the next ten years. Despite such assertions, it should be understood that within the Christian sphere at least one other group claims the distinction of being religion's most dynamic contemporary element. Paradoxically, the claimant is one with which the psychiatrically oriented Church would have the least in common.

Heralded by *Life* as "The Third Force in Christendom," this informal grouping, the magazine noted in a recent article,[1] is comprised of:

[1] June 9, 1958.

"fringe sects"—those marked, in the extreme, by shouting revivalists, puritanical preachers of doomsday, faith healers, jazzy gospel singers. Six million Americans, plus 14,000,000 in other lands, are in its ranks as members of about 100 church groups. They range from the emotional Pentecostals to the sober Adventists. Their churches may be converted stores or 2,000-seat edifices. Most of the third-force groups disagree widely with each other and look with disapproval on each other's way of worship. But they share a common spiritual aim: to return, in deliberate imitation, to the intent and practices of the early Christian Church. Their uncomplicated theology is based on a literal interpretation of the Bible . . .

In an accompanying analysis to this third force, which he describes as "the most extraordinary religious phenomenon of our time," Dr. Henry P. Van Dusen, president of Union Seminary, credits its strengths:

Its groups preach a direct biblical message readily understood. They commonly promise an immediate, life-transforming experience of the living God-in-Christ which is far more significant to the many individuals than the version of it normally found in conventional churches. They directly approach people . . . and do not wait for them to come to church. They have great spiritual ardor. . . . They shepherd their converts in an intimate, sustaining group fellowship: a feature of every vital Christian renewal since the Holy Spirit descended on the disciples at the first Pentecost. They place strong emphasis upon the Holy Spirit—so neglected by many traditional Christians—as the immediate, potent presence of God both in each human soul and in the Christian fellowship. Above all, they expect their followers to practice an active, untiring, seven-day-a-week Christianity.

Dr. Van Dusen also catalogues the group's faults:

Its intellectual outlook is quite limited. For the most part it is blithely indifferent to scientific and historical advances including the proven results of modern inquiry into the writing of the

Bible and the development of the church. Its Christian message tends to be so simple as to be incomplete. Its spirit is all too often narrow, bigoted, and intolerant.

How irresistible or lasting an attraction a movement with flaws of such magnitude will have for Christians, generally, can perhaps be seen in an historical context, Dr. Van Dusen suggests. He points out that rather than a new phenomenon, the third force is a contemporary manifestation of the protest element that has always existed in Christianity (and elsewhere, to be sure), whose function has always been to rebel "from real or alleged faults in older churches." Are the protest groups discounted as "fringe sects"? Not if one has any respect for history, Dr. Van Dusen suggests.

The word "sect" was coined historically to designate and disparage those countless small, radical, and originally despised expressions of the Reformation impulse—the Baptist, Congregationalist, Quaker, Mennonite, Methodist, Disciples, and many others. These sprang up alongside the largest Reformation churches (the Lutherans, Presbyterians, Anglicans) and are now great churches themselves.

Any impression, therefore, that the great quest for a corollary between religion and psychiatry occurs equally through all the branches of our three major faiths must be banished, because it is contrary to fact.

It is well worth repeating that much of the movement toward a psychiatrically oriented religion occurs within those Protestant groups that, traditionally, are receptive to change. Most of the "conversions" to a God of love from one exclusively of judgment, for example, have come from the Protestant element. On the other hand, to say that an improper emphasis on a judgmental God has been an exclusively Protestant fault would also be contrary to fact. As we have seen, some rabbis and priests who have pursued a legalistic theology have also been enlightened through encounters with psychiatric insights.

It would be even worse to conclude that because many religious professionals have been guilty of theological distortions religion should be measured by its errors. There are many skeptics today who are content to dismiss religion from their lives on the basis of a childhood contact, in which, because of inadequate instruction, they were unable to comprehend religion's adult resources, or on the basis of some other unfortunate encounter in which they drew from the antics of a poor theologian the idea that all religion was juvenile, coercive, or unrealistic.

Such a conclusion makes just as much sense as one that assumes that the science of physics has advanced no further than what we learned of it in high school. In religion, as in physics, where we stop others go on. Any lazy skeptic who would trouble himself to take a new look at the products of the minds of our contemporary theologians would be profoundly impressed.

In sophisticated religious circles, the idea of a vindictively judgmental God is on the level of counting on one's fingers with quantum theory, historically interesting but essentially worthless for present use. "Recalling men to a God of love," notes Dr. Seward Hiltner of the University of Chicago, "not trying to win merit by picayunish moralities . . . is found in all our high religions when true to themselves, especially in Judaism and Christianity. To fall into other beliefs has always been poor theology, no matter whether it be ministers or anyone else who do the falling. . . .

"Both Christianity and Judaism have always been aware that idolatry, setting small and unworthy gods in place of the true God, could infiltrate their lines like the Trojan horse. . . . I would contend that only the man who believes deeply that God loves him, apart from anything he has or has not done, can 'fear' God in the proper sense—namely, stand in awe before the majesty of that love. In this sense the religious message is of both fear and love, but the fear without the love has no religious meaning."

Just as broad as the range of viewpoints within beliefs is the range of motivation for accepting or rejecting a synthesis between religion and psychiatry. Many clergymen who accept psychiatric insight for use in their ministries accuse those who don't with fearing for their own existence. Says a Los Angeles hospital chaplain, himself an Episcopalian: "If I got up in a group of Episcopal ministers in this area and said, 'Do you believe adultery is a sin or symptom?' they'd say, 'What's the matter with him? He used to be religious.' They're afraid to water down this thing called sin. If they do, they'll lose control."

While this sort of explanation is applicable in a number of cases, considerable opposition is based on a much more reasonable level. Many religionists, even some who embrace psychiatric insights, are gravely worried that concern with the emotional health of worshipers will smudge up their activities so badly that the clergy will forget about theology, and religion will be lost. Carried to its extreme, the embracing of psychiatry by religion could find the country with thousands of clinics and no churches.

Professor George T. Hedley of Mills College typifies this concern. He points to the increasing importance seminaries are giving to clinical training for their students, and he worries that classical theological education is being neglected. The enthusiasm for counseling ministries could turn the seminary into nothing but a training school. Says Professor Hedley: "There is a danger that the minister will not do the *other* things he ought to do."

Critics from the ranks of pastoral psychology itself challenge the motives of many clergymen who embrace the "new" religion. In this argument, spirituality is seen as having been supplanted by opportunity. A biting analysis in this regard is offered by Rabbi Robert Katz, director of the Department of Human Relations at Hebrew Union College in Cincinnati. "I think many religionists are on the run. They're worried. They ask, 'Who needs us? What do we have to offer?' Let's face it. We wooed the psychiatrists. Religionists worried about their place may have reached out to psychiatry as a new way of finding justification for the role of the pastor."

It is true that many clergymen have turned to psychiatry out of a personal need. In a few instances this need is the very one that would lead any emotionally disturbed individual to psychiatry—a wish to straighten out an emotional problem. But in most cases where there has been a need, the need has been to secure a usefulness and importance for oneself where neither has been before.

"A lot of these men whose religion is bankrupt grab hold of counseling as something to make themselves useful," notes Counseling Expert Reuel Howe. Where such a motivation is present, there is a tendency for the clergymen involved to overplay their hand. They lose sight almost entirely of the fact that as advocates of a spiritual understanding of the universe they have something special to offer. As a result, while they may help people who need specific help for specific problems, they do nothing—either from lack of time or of resources—for the great majority of people whose craving need is for an ethical approach to existence. Recall, for a moment, the assertion of Rabbi Fred Hollander that "most people are not neurotic." If one accepts his observation, one must also see that any attempt by clergymen to preoccupy themselves with neurotic problems would obviously be a distortion of the worst kind. What Rabbi Hollander and others would like to have from depth psychology are tools to make religion something more than a social outlet

for older people and something more than a force to make
bigots out of children. Properly understood, religion, they
fervently believe, can give the baffled and spiritually im-
poverished mortal a richer life by helping him to understand
the anxieties of being.

The application of psychiatric insights to theology is
a high form of art that requires considerable study and
sound orientation. If a clergyman's clinical training is not
integrated with his other studies, those who know contend
that a dangerous situation can result. "I've seen this thing
sometimes take away people's faith without giving them
another," one minister avers. On the other hand, a clergyman
who has applied his training in depth psychology to his
ministry so enthusiastically that he shuts out theology could
conceivably turn his parishioners from worship of God to
worship of psychiatry. Then the church does become a clinic,
even though the clergyman has no right to treat people
beyond a pastoral counseling level.

In all fairness to some clergymen who find themselves
more lay psychologists than theologians these days, it must
be said that they are frequently forced into this position
by their parishioners. This being the age of psychology,
church members, like everyone else, are anxious to discover
what's in it for them. When they hear that their minister has
been trained to help them, they go to him—and if he is not
prepared to deal with them in an almost professional manner,
he is in trouble. One Long Beach, California, minister sums
up the reason neatly: "Counseling? You're just driven to
it if you want to fulfill a function in the community."

Finally, there are such variations, at times, in religious
belief and needs within the same faiths that insensitive
attempts at applying psychiatric insights to religion, while
frequently meeting with success, can sometimes lead to
problems. Religious beliefs, like national allegiances, are

guarded with zeal and passion. If they are to be changed, where change would be to the good, there is an imperative need to go slow. All too often, however, the eager minister goes so fast he gets into trouble.

Exactly this happened to a young minister in a small Southern California industrial town, who for obvious reasons wishes to remain anonymous. Several years ago he became active as a layman in a church whose minister was psychiatrically oriented. He then went into the ministry himself and served for a time with the source of his inspiration. Then he struck out on his own, eventually arriving at the small California town. By this time he had gone into analysis, and his own methods had become dominated by depth insights.

Blissfully he began to give sermons with psychological overtones. He told his congregation that personal adjustment was a part of religious growth. He used words they had never heard before.

He might have gotten by, except for one thing. He instituted a counseling program and urged anyone with a problem to come in and talk it over.

The reaction was not pleasant. "What's he pryin' for?" one woman muttered. "What'll he do with all those notes he makes?"

The young man had correctly gauged the congregation to a point. Half of the parishioners were willing to see science and theology draw from one another. Another quarter questioned the relationship, but did nothing to inhibit it. What the young minister did not correctly gauge was the vociferousness of the final quarter that didn't like the idea a bit.

Once grown, the resentment was organized. Meetings were called to discuss the new man who would not preach the Word or lay down the Law. At one meeting emotions ran so high that one woman called the young minister "unchristian."

Finally the board of elders of the church bowed to pressure, and recommended that the minister's work be confined to a youth program and to limited counseling, again with young people.

There is more to be drawn from this incident than the defeat of a young minister whose foot was too heavy and pace too fast. Perhaps a more significant bellwether for the fate of religion and psychiatry was that four other churches, hearing of his difficulties, urged him to resign his post and accept a position with them.

It is conceivable, of course, that some counterforce may arise—and if we are to take the story of the "third force" literally, may already have arisen—to cause a conservative reaction in religion. A badly frightened populace, for example, could make demands upon its churches for a stern, vindictive God, a rigid theology, and a legalistic morality that at least says to a drifting man, "This is where you stand."

It may also be that there will be occasional setbacks to the cause of religion and psychiatry. Consider, for example, a situation in which a denomination elects a new national chairman every several years. Of the candidates, one may favor the attempt by the group's division of education to incorporate psychiatric insights into Sunday-school and adult studies. But suppose another candidate is from a faction that is violently opposed to what has been going on. His election could serve to undo all that had been done in the last decade —and the situation described could fit more than one United States denomination today.

But despite the possibility of setbacks, either temporary or profound, there is no overlooking the clear, marked, constant tendency of religion toward the insights of psychiatry.

Whatever the fate of the counterforces, the prospect is clearly for the growth of the psychological element to continue. If there were nothing more than an advocate here and there in the ranks of the clergy, the trend could be dismissed as something without staying power. But the opposite is true. The men influenced by psychiatry are the theologians whose books the young students will read, the professors whose courses they will take. They are the directors of education whose materials they will distribute for use in Sunday schools, the teaching experts who will train the religious-education instructors who, in turn, will teach in the minister's parish. They are the psychiatrists and chaplains who will give courses to clergymen. They are everywhere they should be if, as seems likely, they are to have a lasting and significant effect on the minds of the future.

Many observers will always see in church patterns an imitation of the main currents of society. Says one critic: "The laity is always teaching the ministry something. Theology has a way of shifting with the winds, even when it doesn't know exactly which way the winds are shifting." Yet others, confronted with such an opinion, can be equally bitter. They swear that psychiatry is the very thing the Church has needed for centuries to put itself over with people.

Even if the embracing of psychiatry was an expedient, are expedients always bad? the advocates argue. Here, clearly, if the minister was trying to justify his own existence, he was also making himself more effective. Perhaps, as Samuel Blizzard suggests, the development arose out of "frustration rather than insight." But Mr. Blizzard himself points out that "ministers were finding it more and more a problem to be effective in their work, if they were to continue using only the traditional means at hand."

It may well be that many ministers in their zeal are exceeding the bounds of their competence in dealing with emotionally disturbed people. There are ministers giving lay analysis, and unless they are lay analysts as well as ministers, the complaints against them are valid. An untrained man is simply not competent to handle the problems that

arise in deep therapy, such as what to do about the demanding love he creates for himself in the troubled person, who
sees in him someone who truly cares.

But these excesses, while they exist, are infrequent. More
and more of the training being given to clergymen in pastoral
counseling today is, to judge by its origins, as good as can be
had. Its positive contributions far exceed the negative. The
young minister is taught to see a parishioner in a new relationship, as someone who is not to be told, but understood,
as someone to whom he must listen and counsel with, support
rather than scold. For the healthy individual, it puts a new
warm concept of God within reach.

For the emotionally troubled individual, furthermore, it
puts a new resource at his disposal. And in the final sense,
where else can most troubled people go? Who will care for
them if a trained and sympathetic clergyman won't? Recall
for a moment the figures cited by Father Bier. We have 650,-
000 patients in mental hospitals; they equal the number of
all other hospital patients combined. One out of every
twelve children born today will probably go to a mental
institution at some time in his life, and this ratio could increase as life gets tougher and tougher. In World War II we
lost the services of 3,000,000 men because they were suffering
from some form of emotional disorder. And the National
Association for Mental Health asserts that 9,000,000 Americans are suffering from some form of mental or emotional
disorder.

It is preposterous to assume that 9,000,000 Americans are
ever going to be under the care of psychiatrists. The charge
for a psychiatrist's hour is still about as large as most weekly
food bills for a family of four. There are no injections or
other miracle processes by which the decade or more of study
required by aspirant psychiatrists can be given in less time
and with less cost to the candidates. We can therefore be

assured that the number of psychiatrists will remain small, the fees large, and the available assistance far less than the need for some time to come.

But the need is not diminished. There are millions of Americans with problems, millions with the dim beginnings of neurosis. If not helped and supported in some way, many of them might one day require confinement. Are these people to be ignored? Recall Father Devlin's cry: "I get fourteen, fifteen, sixteen referrals a day. I can't take any more. Where am I going to send these people?"

Many problems can be solved with the proper help. Often they are not so complicated that they can't be adequately handled by a sensitive, concerned clergyman who has had the proper training. If he is accessible, why shouldn't he help? Certainly he should not exceed his bounds, but neither should he ignore the clear needs of his pastorate for a type of assistance that is religious in the highest sense. As Dr. Dana Farnsworth of Harvard University so aptly put it:

"This is not a question of competing. The amount of human suffering is so great that all our combined efforts are weak in comparison to the need."

14.

"I MIGHT SAY YOU'RE PLAYING WITH FIRE"

PLANES of the El Al Airline flying to Israel land today at an airport in Lod, not far from Tel Aviv. Twenty-one hundred years ago Lod was known as Lydda, and it was there that a group of Jewish scholars is said to have held one of history's most epic arguments. Lasting two and one-half years, its concern was but this single question: "Ought God to have created the world?"

At the end of the argument a majority of the scholars, keenly sensing the preposterous difficulties that were to assail man in his attempt to exist in God's creation, decided that it would have been simpler if God had not created the world in the first place. They made one important amendment, however. They said that since God *had* created the world, man should try to make the most of it.

For better or for worse, man has been trying ever since.

The battle has been marked by high points of enlightenment and low points of active self-destruction, and inasmuch as each of these periods is distinguished by some striking event or a new direction of thought, historians are pretty well in accord as to which was which and when. The Renaissance, to take just one example, is said to have begun in 1453 when the Turks took Constantinople, the Byzantine Empire came to an end, and the first great period of modern thought began.

What of our own time? Out of all history, will it achieve distinction as a period of development and discovery that will be picked over by future scholars? Even an ordinary man can see that our chances for significance are excellent, for whereas most distinguished periods are marked by a single discovery of epochal proportions, ours has already seen the birth of two.

One of these, of course, is that the atom can be split, with great consequences. The other is that the man who splits the atom is infinitely more complex than he seems to be and that within the incredible warren of his unconscious mind runs, among other things, a persistent desire to punish himself. With all the billions of years the universe is said to have existed, it is unfortunate that the two discoveries should have occurred within forty years of one another. As a result, man may have found out about himself too late to avoid his own destruction.

There is no civilized man today who is not aware of the capability mankind has achieved to assign his remnants to an age of blackness. How is it that he has permitted his science so to outdistance his ethics? How is it that if he were somehow to resurrect the scholars of Lod, he would scare the daylights out of them with his airplanes but impress them not at all with his manners? How is it that in reaching an age of incipient total destruction man has achieved no philosophy of certain total being?

Religion, it is said, has failed. Christianity, to take the most popular example, has had 2,000 years to provide man with a workable ethic, but that many years later man is still working his way to oblivion.

In many practical respects religion *has* failed to bring sense to life. While most of us dutifully go to Sunday school in our early years, we learn to think of religious content much as we learn to walk; after we have learned the rudiments, we cease to think consciously about them. We no more consider what we are saying than we consider the movement of one foot after the other.

But learning to think in terms of love and acceptance is a lot more involved than learning to walk, and few of us ever make the higher effort. Indeed, few of us have the resources available in terms of teachers who care to reach us, or books we can comprehend, to make the achievement of a deep understanding of our own commitment to creation a possibility. The dismaying discovery by service chaplains in World War II that most young American men had no religious vocabulary, no understanding of God in relation to themselves, and only an intuitive and negative understanding of the beliefs in which they were raised—that they were, in plain words, religious illiterates—is proof that religion has failed to put forth convincingly the resource we need.

What we need is an *adult ethic,* and if religion fails to give it to us, the tragedy will be keen. Because the ethic is there. There is an ideal surging through our Judeo-Christian heritage that in the happiest of circumstances could catch ethics up to science in time to lift man's hand from the ultimate button. Both religious and psychological, it is therefore ethical and applicable. It is the ancient, simple, and virtually inoperative idea that love can conquer hate.

Religion spoke first of love. But history may say that psychiatry, in our time, at last caused love to be understood.

There are many virtuous things of which an advocate could boast in assessing psychiatry's contribution to religion. Much could be made about the alleviation of human suffering that might result from the ministrations of thousands of clergymen who have been trained to deal with people in distress. There is little question, furthermore, that with this very same training clergymen will come to an understanding of people that will enable them to better serve as guides to a fuller life. Nor does there seem to be any question that as religion learns more about the sensitivities of the mind, it will at the same time learn not to make demands on human conduct that have no relation to theology, none to ethics, and certainly none to reality. The separation of the ideal from the attainable will become more and more narrow, and man will cease to be sick with guilt because he was unable to achieve what he never could.

Nor, the pursuit of self-understanding being the most rewarding game in which man can engage, is there any question that he will find the job easier and the goal more accessible because of the enrichment of the theological vocabulary by psychological insights.

All of these virtues could easily result from an age in which new understanding about the nature of man has turned on the lights in many dark minds.

But exciting though these developments may be, they are potentially as nothing compared to the possibilities inherent in man's new understanding of love.

He has learned that babies who are fed but not held will probably die. He has learned that children who are deprived of love become our delinquents, psychotics, and criminals, our miserable millions beset by emotional problems. Man knows now for the first time in his existence that he actually *needs* love, not for the sensation it brings to his body, but for the sanity it assures his mind.

The question remains whether, sensing, at last, his imperative need for love, man yet knows how to get it.

The answer is that he does. Protestant, Catholic, or Jew, this is his debt to psychiatry. He knows now, because he has seen the proof, that he gets true sustaining love by loving when it's tough.

He loves the people he can't stand, the sinners and the

unlovables. With this love, he communicates a power that redeems the sinner and creates a counterthrust of love that completes his own life. Psychiatry proved that unquestioning acceptance is the absolutely essential beginning of redemption for the man who, unloved in the first place, became someone no one could stand. What has not been so well emphasized is that it is essential to our *own* survival that we accept others for what they are. *We* cannot get the love *we* need to redeem ourselves unless we love others in a way that wins their love.

This is what the churches and synagogues mean now when they speak with new urgency of accepting the sinners in their midst. Where many of them have always cried for an embracing love, they have now learned that there are consequences for failing to accept others without question. This is why churches that once demanded adherence to an encumbered set of laws see now that this quest for total conformity is irreligious, simply because it is irrelevant. Illumination is the word for what has happened, and in cases where illumination was badly needed, the light, by contrast, is intense.

We will now see whether religion, understanding the dynamics of love, understanding its own resources, will apply this understanding and these resources to our monstrous situation and save us from our own misguided hands.

Is it too farfetched to suppose that religion could succeed? That ours could be the age when we might finally achieve an adult ethic? While most of our attention is drawn to examples of self-destruction, it is nevertheless evident that ours is a century for self-enhancement like no other in history. If we have more power to obliterate the world, we have, if we dare, far more power to put heaven on earth. We are extending life spans. We are licking disease. Begrudgingly, perhaps, but nonetheless inexorably, we are beginning to spread our bounty. Assuming that our science and our vision are agile enough to surmount the current population explosion, we can look to the day when demagogues will no longer turn rumbling bellies to roaring wars.

An age of enough would change many things, but not everything. It would not change man's concern for himself. No matter how much he has he will continue to raven for more. Until he is convinced that lusting for his neighbor's yard is not the way to happiness, he is not going to change.

What will change him? Many say nothing, and it is far easier to assume so than to seek answers. But people can be affected. They do respond, if enough power is used to persuade them. Will psychiatry generate such power? Hardly. Psychiatry, by itself, is too specific, too restricted. The need, on the other hand, is too general, too abundant.

The solution has to be a good deal simpler, a good deal more accessible. In the final analysis, because there is no other place from which it can come, it has to be religion—which in its highest form is simply an organized, systematic quest for the meaning of one's being, for worthy answers to the vagaries of life.

Being religious means being concerned. Perhaps this is why so many Americans, emerging from a period of religious impoverishment and skepticism, are returning to churches in droves. They are looking for salvation when, for the first time in history, salvation has a specific literal meaning that makes the spiritual idea of redemption a reality.

But can religion provide this adult ethic by which we can bring sense to life?

It can if it distributes the best that it's got. There is reason to suspect that it isn't doing so now.

Ordinary religious adherents today are not getting the best of their faiths. Too many of them are taught a second-class creed by second-class thinkers. Somehow the best thinking never gets to them. Most Protestants have never heard of

Tillich. Few Jews understand Buber. Few Catholics realize
that the science they disparage is the same that their late Pope
praised.

This is terrible. Why haven't the advanced ideas about the
applicability of religion to our human situation been expressed meaningfully for the man who moves his lips as he
reads? When the *Saturday Evening Post* began a series called
"Adventures of the Mind" not long ago, it may have isolated
the reason:

> For some little time [it wrote], we *Post* editors have been
> deeply disturbed by the obvious—and obviously dangerous—
> chasm that separates the intellectuals of our nation from the
> millions of citizens whose attitudes and opinions determine
> national policy and set the standards of national behavior.
>
> The intellectual, or "egghead" (as we carelessly brand him),
> has deep reservations about the ordinary layman. He feels that we
> don't understand him, or respect him, or reward his labors—that
> we give to the crooner, the comedian, the halfback, the allegiance
> of our minds and our pocketbooks. And so he goes his cloistered
> way—toiling quietly in his laboratory, at his easel, typewriter, or
> blackboard, communicating chiefly with his colleagues through
> lectures and scholarly journals.[1]

Ideas are as useful as they are applicable, no more, no less.
By themselves, lacking a clamorous human voice, they are
essentially worthless.

We can no longer afford a condition in which men of
ideas come to love their thoughts so much that they never
put them to the common man, whose need is greatest of all.
The best minds of religion must somehow convey to mankind
the ferment in all three major faiths today, that true worth
is established by the willingness to take the first step, make
the first gesture and, if necessary, the first sacrifice.

[1] "Adventures of the Mind," April 26, 1958.

It is nonsense to think that, religion reawakened to its own resources, there will now be a mass conversion to the principle of accepting the unacceptables. It is folly to think that this ancient idea, dynamically acted on in our own century, will open the arms of the whites to the colored, the communists to capitalists, the haves to the have-nots. But conversion is one thing and construction is another, and the start made by many churches and synagogues in the United States today toward a deeper understanding of man's need of his fellow man could be the true beginning of redemption. For while it remains a question as to which will occur first, destruction or discovery, it is possible that the age of the ultimate weapon could also become the age of the ultimate ethic, when we come to an understanding of why we so actively seek to destroy not only each other, but ourselves. We may yet learn, before it's too late, that the same whim that sends us to doom can be better served by loving what we hate.

It's an old idea with new force. To anyone who tries it, perhaps it is well to recall the parson's warning:

"I might say that you're playing with fire."